Understanding and Working with Parents of Children in Long-Term Foster Care

Understanding and Working with Parents of Children in Long-Term Foster Care

Gillian Schofield and Emma Ward

Jessica Kingsley *Publishers*
London and Philadelphia

First published in 2011
by Jessica Kingsley Publishers
116 Pentonville Road
London N1 9JB, UK
and
400 Market Street, Suite 400
Philadelphia, PA 19106, USA

www.jkp.com

Library of Congress Cataloging in Publication Data
Schofield, Gillian, 1951-
    Understanding and working with parents of children in long-term foster care / Gillian Schofield and Emma Ward.
        p. cm.
    Includes bibliographical references and index.
    ISBN 978-1-84905-026-5 (alk. paper)
    1. Parenting. 2. Foster children. 3. Parent and child. 4. Foster home care. I. Ward, Emma. II. Title.
    HQ755.85.S363 2011
    649'.1--dc22
                                2010022253

British Library Cataloguing in Publication Data
A CIP catalogue record for this book is available from the British Library

ISBN 978 1 84905 026 5

Printed and bound in Great Britain by
MPG Books Group

Contents

Acknowledgements

We would like to thank the Economic and Social Research Council for funding this research. We have also very much valued our collaboration with our colleagues running parallel studies at the University of Bergen, Norway (Bente Moldestad, Dag Skilbred and Toril Havik) and at the University of Gothenburg, Sweden (Ingrid Höjer). We also thank Julie Young, Senior Research Associate at the University of East Anglia, for helping with the analysis.

We are very grateful indeed to the social workers who contacted parents for us and also gave of their own time to attend focus groups for this project.

But most of all we need to thank the parents who talked to us so openly, so helpfully and so movingly about loss, separation and the experience of being parents of children growing up in foster care.

1.

Introduction: Legal, Policy and Research Context

The family situations that result in children coming into care are rarely simple, and those children who need to remain in foster care through childhood and adolescence will generally come from highly troubled families with multiple problems. Their parents have often had their own childhood histories of poverty and deprivation, abuse and neglect, followed by adult lives marred by domestic violence, drug and alcohol misuse and mental health difficulties (Schofield *et al.* 2000; Sinclair 2005). These risk factors not only increase the likelihood of parents being unable to care for their children safely, but also continue to affect parents once children are removed into foster care. Parents thus face a difficult path if they are to learn to live with the reality of their loss and retain some role as parents to their children.

This book is designed to help social workers understand the range of parents' experiences, reactions and attitudes to the loss of their children, from the earliest days of parenting the children at home, through and after the separation into foster care, and on into the teenage years, when young people may have been apart from their parents for much of their childhood. The aim is to promote social work practice that recognises and supports parents as 'people with needs of their own' (Children Act 1989), but that is also child focussed. The potential influence of parents on the stability and developmental outcomes for their children will continue to be significant through to adulthood. So it is essential that whatever the nature of the parents' history or current involvement in the lives of their foster children, attention be paid to managing that role and relationship in a way that is as constructive and rewarding as possible, for parents and for children.

The book will draw primarily on a detailed study of the experiences and views of parents of children growing up in foster care, but it also includes the perceptions of social workers on their work with parents. This introductory chapter will first consider the legal, policy and practice context and, in particular, what we know from research about the parents of children in foster care.

Parents and the stability and well-being of foster children

The stability and well-being of children growing up in foster care will be affected by many factors in the child, the foster family and the services that support them, but one very important factor will be the nature of their ongoing relationship with their birth parents and families (Beek and Schofield 2004 a and b; Biehal *et al.* 2010; Cleaver 2000; Farmer, Moyes and Liscombe 2004; Höjer 2007; Schofield 2009; Schofield *et al.* 2000; Schofield and Stevenson 2009; Selwyn *et al.* 2006; Sinclair 2005; Sinclair *et al.* 2007; Thoburn, Norford and Rashid 2000; Thorpe 1980). Yet the links between the parents' continuing involvement in their children's lives and outcomes are not simple. Addressing this issue requires a flexible approach that takes into account the full range of parental involvement and attitude, interacting with the full range of children, foster carers and social work practice.

Although the role of parents is recognised by social workers to be a significant issue for fostered children and young people, the experience of parents and models of social work practice with parents are not well represented in research (Alpert 2005), just as they are not in policy and practice guidance. There is thus generally a shortage of information on parents' experiences, particularly as their role evolves over the years of separation as their children grow up in foster families. Thoburn (1996) has argued the need for a model of social work practice that recognises the dual importance to children in long-term foster care of their relationships with parents and with foster carers, and which values the potential contribution of parents, even when their primary role may be to 'care about' rather than 'care for' children.

There are particular challenges in defining parents' experience and role when children are subject to a long-term or permanent foster care plan. Here the foster carers will be seen as the primary source of attachment, nurturance and protection and the parents' role as parents while apart from their children is often unclear and will vary over the years. It is important therefore to track the evolution of the parent role, as children first become settled in the long-term foster home and over time may grow closer to foster carers and grow away from parents. These changes can shift the balance in parental identities for parents and for carers.

There will be a range of potentially positive or negative parental influences. At the positive end of this range, parents may accept the child being in foster care over time and support the child's stability and well-being in the foster home. At the negative end of the range, parents may make it very difficult for the child to settle and for the foster carers to parent the child. Most parents will fall somewhere within this range and their position may change at various points during the child's growing up years. Whatever their position, their beliefs, attitudes and behaviour will be influencing the extent to which the foster family placement can be successful in meeting the child's needs. Work with parents, as well as work with foster carers and with children in relation to the birth family, can thus play an important role in promoting the child's well-being.

The legal context

The parents' experience and role will be affected by the legal context of parenting responsibilities for the foster child, since this will dictate, at least to some degree, how their role is defined.

The majority of children subject to a long-term plan in foster care are likely to be subject to a Care Order (s31 Children Act 1989). In this context, parents who have legal parental responsibility for the child do not lose their parental responsibility, but the local authority is also given parental responsibility and has the right to limit the parents' exercise of their parental responsibility in order to safeguard and promote the welfare of the child. However, a minority of children in planned long-term foster care will be accommodated with parental agreement (section 20 Children Act 1989), when legal parental responsibility remains entirely with parents. This may occur, for example, when children with disability can no longer be cared for by a birth parent, who then asks for the child to be looked after or perhaps more surprisingly, when a child is rejected or abandoned by their parents (Schofield 2000; Schofield et al. 2000).

There are no officially published figures for the proportion of children in planned long-term foster care who are on care orders or are accommodated under section 20, because plans are not recorded in a way that can be aggregated locally or nationally. Schofield *et al.* (2000) found that the proportion of children under section 20 in their sample of 52 planned long-term foster care placements in 1997–1998 was 33 per cent, which reflected the overall figures for the care population at the time (DH 1999). An analysis of 230 planned long-term foster care cases in 2006/2007 in six local authorities (Schofield *et al.* in preparation) has shown that only 12 per cent were accommodated under section 20, in the context of a national figure of 30 per cent of all looked after children (DfES 2007). This may suggest that local authorities are taking stronger steps to gain parental responsibility through a care order for children for whom the care plan will be long-term care.

A survey of local authority and independent fostering providers regarding long-term planning in foster care (Schofield and Ward *et al.* 2008) suggested that although for most agencies the s20 legal status is no official barrier to long-term placements, and some s20 placements work very well, there was sometimes concern about how decisions about children and the role of birth parents are managed in these particular long-term placements. Key here is the fact that the local authority's role as corporate parent in relation to accommodated children is covered by the Children Act 1989 section 22, which sets out the local authority's 'duty to safeguard the welfare of all looked after children'. This duty must include those children for whom they do not have parental responsibility, although social workers often feel disempowered in the absence of legal parental responsibility (Schofield 2000).

Whatever the legal status of the child, the expectation in the Children Act 1989 is that local authorities will wherever possible work in *partnership with parents*, a principle that applies not only when children are at home, but also when they are looked after. The principle of taking into account the needs of birth families has been reinforced by the provisions of the Adoption and Children Act 2002, which include support plans and services for birth parents among the post-adoption support requirements. If parents are to be entitled to a range of support services even after their legal role as the child's parents has been ended by the court in adoption, it must be obvious that parents of children in long-term foster care should also be entitled to support. In foster care it is even more likely to be the case that social work with parents can promote the well-being of the child, since contact is taken for granted in most cases and parents have the potential to be actively influential in children's lives. However, although support for parents of children in foster care is assumed to be available, in practice this may not be the case (Alpert 2005; Kapp and Propp 2002; Kapp and Vela 2004). This raises special concerns where there is no requirement for support plans to be agreed when placements are confirmed as permanent (Schofield and Ward *et al.* 2008).

The involvement of parents of children in foster care in their children's lives is likely to be in two main arenas laid down in law and procedure. The first is that of *decision making and review*, since whatever the legal status of the foster child, parents retain parental responsibility. There is therefore an expectation that they will be involved in certain kinds of decision making and, in particular, will play a part in the six-monthly Looked After Children (LAC) review process. It will be for the Independent Reviewing Officer (IRO), a role introduced in 2004 under section 118 of the Adoption and Children Act 2002, to ensure that parents and other relatives are consulted during the review process and/or at review meetings in relation to important decisions that affect the child. However, there is no guidance, and indeed there is a general lack of clarity, about whether the role of parents in decision making and in the LAC review process or meetings should change in any way once a decision has been made that foster care will be the permanence plan for the child (Schofield and Ward *et al.* 2008), just as there is no guidance or clarity on the role of the social worker in long-term cases in relation to work with birth parents (discussed further in later chapters).

The second arena of expected parental involvement in the child's life will be that of *contact*. The Children Act 1989 s34 set out the principle of a 'presumption of reasonable contact' between the child and birth parents (and other relatives or significant people where appropriate). This principle has to be considered in the light of the overall principle of the priority to be given to the best interests and welfare of the child, also contained in the Children Act 1989. So contact should be seen as for the child's benefit rather than as a parental right. However, this distinction oversimplifies a complex situation in which rights are less of an issue than the quality of relationships (Cleaver 2000; Schofield and Stevenson 2009; Sinclair 2005). Although it may not be a formally recognised *right* of the parent to have contact with their child in care, the relationship between the child and the parent will rely on the way in which they think about each other, the extent to which their lives are connected and the quality of that connection. Whether contact is direct or indirect, frequent or infrequent, supervised or unsupervised, constructive or damaging, the quality of the relationship between parent and child as it evolves over the years will depend to no small degree on the quality of contact.

Contact with the child in foster care is therefore often the issue that most influences and is influenced by the nature of the parents' role in the foster child's life. This is true for all types of placement (Cleaver 2000; Macaskill 2002), but is especially relevant for children and young people in long-term foster care, where contact may be at any level, from once a week to twice a year (Beek and Schofield 2004b) and the reasons for these differences may not always be clear. There are few cases where children in foster care, including long-term foster care, have no contact with any family members and where this does occur it is most likely to be because birth relatives have withdrawn and do not take up arrangements for contact rather than by court order (Beek and Schofield 2004b; Cleaver 2000; Farmer *et al.* 2004; Sinclair, Baker and Wilson 2005). So contact is likely to be happening and all parents and children, carers and social workers need to work together to make contact a constructive part of the child's placement and life.

Sinclair (2005, p.94), reviewing the research on contact in foster care, concluded that because contact has the potential to be beneficial or harmful in different situations, 'A wide view needs to be taken about its potential and a lively eye kept to its dangers'. Research is now much clearer about the need for careful assessments to ensure that contact meets the child's needs in permanent placements (Neil and Howe 2004), but whether it is beneficial or harmful in practice will depend significantly not only on the quality of the assessment of the child's needs and work with children and carers, but also on the quality of work that is done with the parents.

Policy and practice on permanence in foster care and the role of parents

Very relevant as a context for parental involvement with their children in foster care is the development of national and local policy on 'permanence' and its impact on practice. The goal of permanent family placements that offer long-term stability and family membership through childhood has been part of social work practice and care planning in the courts since the mid 1980s (Maluccio *et al.* 1986; Thoburn, Murdoch and O'Brien 1986). During the subsequent years, there has been far less of a policy commitment to long-term foster care as a permanence option than adoption, but it has nevertheless been described as 'a legitimate permanence option' in *Every Child Matters* (DfES 2003, p.45), and was, for example, included in a list of permanence options in *Care Matters: Time for Change* (DfES 2007, p.54) and in *Care Planning, Placements and Case Review Guidance and Regulations* (DCSF 2010:12). However, where long-term fostering *is* the permanence plan, there are no specific expectations laid down nationally (unlike for adoption) as to how this will be achieved procedurally (Lowe and Murch *et al.* 2001; Schofield and Ward *et al.* 2008), nor are there any defined implications of this type of foster placement for the future of the parents' role.

Research approaches the issue of permanence in foster care from a number of different perspectives, reflecting the range of issues that affect practice. Sinclair *et al.* (2005) concluded that there were four different kinds of permanence in foster care: objective permanence, subjective permanence, enacted permanence and uncontested permanence. It is possible to argue that parents may be having some impact on each. *Objective permanence*, where children have a placement that will last during childhood and provide support in adulthood, may be easier or harder to achieve depending on whether carers or children feel that the parents will support or disrupt the child's continuing place in the foster family in adolescence. *Subjective permanence*, the child's feeling of belonging in the foster family, may be facilitated or threatened by the extent to which parents are able to give emotional permission to the child to feel settled as part of the foster family. *Enacted permanence* is defined in terms of everyone accepting that the child is a foster family member. Although the foster family may be able to offer the child this acceptance, it is also important for the parents to accept the child as a member of the foster family, given the likely continuation of contact. The social worker's ability to work with the child in the foster family and to themselves see this as a 'real family' for the child into the future is important, but will be facilitated by knowing that the parents are accepting it, at least to some degree. Finally, *uncontested permanence*, where the child does not feel a clash of loyalty between foster and birth family, is much more likely to occur if the parents are able to resolve their feelings of loss and explicitly enable or at least allow the child to resolve their different loyalties to both families.

In a study of planning for permanence in foster care (Schofield and Ward *et al.* 2008), we found that there was a great deal of variety, not only in how permanence in foster care was defined and planned, but also in the implications for parents. Many local authorities suggested that the decision to make a 'permanent' or 'long-term' foster care plan for a child (language and concepts vary between local authorities) will depend on the nature of the existing relationship with the parents and the level of contact that is deemed to be in the child's interests. In other authorities, or even for different children in the same authority, it may be argued the other way round, with permanence in foster care becoming the plan and leading to a redefinition of the parents' role, for example by a reduction in contact. These variations in systems are matched by very different approaches in different authorities in the extent to which parents are seen as key decision makers for children in long-term or permanent foster care, regarding issues as wide ranging as haircuts and school trips. Such uncertainty around meanings, procedures and decisions about the role of parents have an impact on the child, but also need to be understood from the parents' point of view.

Schofield *et al.* (2000) interviewed parents as part of their wider study of planned long-term foster care. They found that parents' experiences of permanence planning in foster care reflected the diversity of the circumstances of the separation, ranging from a collaborative plan for children with severe disabilities to be looked after long-term by former respite carers, through to fiercely contested court cases with parental anger at the social work agencies being a dominant theme. Feelings of sadness and loss after the separation were, however, universal, particularly when parents realised that the children would not be returning home. Some parents questioned whether the right help had been offered to them when they needed it, but others recognised that they had not always been good parents or been able to protect their children from abusive partners. For some parents it had been a relief when the children were taken into care. One mother who had been abused herself as a child and admitted being involved in the sexual abuse of her children said that she was glad the cycle of abuse was ending.

Whatever the role or reactions of parents, the place of permanence in policy seems assured. Although the first choice placement will always be the immediate birth family and then wider kinship networks, permanence that involves separating children from families for placement in adoption or foster care will continue to be necessary in some cases. The Government White Paper *Care Matters: Time for Change* (DfES 2007) has stressed the importance of achieving better outcomes for children in care by improving the quality of foster care through to adulthood and by improving the quality of social work practice. It is essential to include in that aspiration for high quality social work practice a commitment to good practice with parents, informed by parents' experiences, as this too will contribute to foster children's well-being and long-term stability.

Loss, stigma and identity

Parents whose children are growing up in foster care face many challenges, but underlying these will be the need to manage the powerful, diverse and often contradictory feelings that arise from their experience of loss. There may be grief for the loss of their children, but also, for some parents, relief that the children are now cared for and thriving. Parents' anger at the loss may be directed at a partner, at a social worker, at a court – or at themselves, with feelings of guilt and regret making it even more difficult to resolve feelings of grief and anger. But additional, and cutting across the task of managing these powerful emotions, will be the parents' struggle over the years of their children's childhood in care to maintain their identity as a parent; an identity that has not been entirely lost but is severely threatened by the care status of their children (Schofield *et al.* 2010).

Previous studies have shown how difficult it can be for parents separated from their children to manage or 'resolve' powerful feelings of loss and grief and anger (Haight *et al.* 2002; Höjer 2007, 2009; Moldestad and Skilbred 2009; Schofield *et al.* 2000). There are useful parallels with Neil's study of parents whose children were adopted from care (Neil 2007), which grouped parents into those who positively accepted the placement, those who were resigned and those who were angry and resistant. These types of parental reaction are recognisable from previous studies of long-term foster care (Schofield *et al.* 2000).

But what is always significant when comparing adoption and foster care is that the adoption order will have removed the legal parental rights and responsibilities of birth parents in a final way that is not the case when children are in foster care. Reaching a state of acceptance and resolution in adoption is, of course, also a complex and evolving process, and may never be fully achieved. But there is no doubt that for parents of children in foster care, the continuation of a legal status as parents and face-to-face contact with their children, combined with the possibility of returning to court to challenge the separation or the contact arrangements, makes the process of 'resolution' and the redefining of parental identity for parents of foster children a very different and ongoing challenge.

Key to understanding the experiences of these particular parents, and a complicating factor in achieving an emotional resolution, is the fact that high expectations of parenthood in society lead inevitably to the stigmatisation of parents who do not meet them, such as parents of children in foster care. The parental identity is a social construction that is also linked to moral judgements, with parents expected to prioritise the needs of their children and judged by society if they appear to have failed to do so (Ribbens McCarthy, Edwards and Gillies 2000). For this group of parents whose children are in foster care, the experience of being judged and therefore of stigma is likely to come from multiple sources. Höjer (2007), for example, found feelings of stigmatisation to be an important issue for mothers who had abused drugs and whose children came into care as a result. These mothers could describe how desperate they felt when they were blamed and criticised not only for using drugs but for 'making the wrong choices', i.e. making drugs their first priority instead of the care of their children. Their value and identity as parents was questioned.

Because parents of children in foster care are at risk of stigma, their situation is such that even their right to grieve the loss of their children and their entitlement to public sympathy may be compromised by what Doka (1989) has described as 'disenfranchised grief', grief that is not culturally acknowledged or supported (see also Robinson 2002). For parents of children in foster care, the loss is both ambiguous and stigmatised: legally, but not practically, they continue to be parents, and managing their grief is complicated by the likelihood that public blame has been attached to them for the loss.

Parents of children in foster care have lost the care of their child and, since this is how the role and identity of parent is most commonly defined, there is a significant *threat to their identity* (Breakwell 1986; Crocker and Quinn 2004). In her research on another group of parents whose identity is threatened, non-resident mothers after divorce and separation, Kielty (2008, 2009) found that there were both private and public tasks to master. The mothers needed ways of coming to terms with the loss of the children and their main caregiving role, but also strategies for sustaining the identity of a (good) mother, privately and publicly, in spite of it. For these non-resident mothers, feelings of grief, loss and anger often interacted with feelings of guilt and regret, with particular problems emerging for identity resolution and self-esteem when mothers lacked a sense of agency about the separation.

The parallels to parents of children in foster care are clear, including the significant question of agency. The complexity of managing strong feelings in relation to their loss, while also managing their threatened identity as parents of fostered children, is an important element in this book.

Cognitive dissonance

One further element in our theoretical understanding of the dilemmas facing parents is their need to manage forms of *cognitive dissonance* (Festinger 1957). This concept suggests that holding contradictory ideas causes psychological stress, raises anxiety and lowers self-esteem. There are two areas of conflict for parents of children in foster care to resolve: the first is the gap or contradiction between how they see themselves as parents and how other people (their families, social workers, courts, neighbours, the community) see them; the second is the contradiction within their own set of beliefs, between seeing themselves as having tried to be a good parent and yet knowing that children had been harmed while in their care. The challenge of reflecting on and resolving these contradictions will occur at all stages as their children grow up in foster families. This will be discussed specifically in Chapter 8. But it is important to be aware from the start of the book that parents are having to develop strategies to manage their experiences of loss and identity at each stage, from the point at which children come into care, through the years that children remain in foster care and even after they leave care.

Social work roles and relationships

The range of complex psychological challenges for parents of children in foster care also has to be managed over time in the context of their relationship with social workers who have responsibilities for the welfare of the child. These social workers are also likely to have powerful and contradictory feelings about their own role; on the one hand, safeguarding children from harmful family environments, but on the other hand separating parents from their children. Social workers are therefore managing their own feelings, sometimes too of sadness and anger, as well as working with those feelings in the parents. For social workers, as for parents, there is a lack of clarity, especially where foster care is a permanent placement, about the appropriate parenting role and identity of the parent in each case. There is also little clarity about the expected social work role in relation to parents of children in long-term foster care (Schofield *et al.* 2010), in contrast to the relative clarity about the social worker's role in relation to the child, which is covered by statute and guidance.

One primary dilemma for social workers will be whether the work with parents is always to be undertaken with the goal of directly or indirectly benefiting the child or whether, as legislation in England (Children Act 1989) suggests, parents have rights to have their own needs recognised and support offered in a spirit of partnership. Put simply, when their primary role is to secure the *child's* well-being, can hard-pressed social workers justify spending time with parents helping them to resolve some of their complex feelings of grief, loss and anger in order to promote the *parents'* well-being? It is, and should be, argued that helping parents, who are often vulnerable adults themselves, to resolve their feelings may enable them to be more constructive in their role as parents, for example, when having contact with their children. But can or should agencies meet parents' entitlement to a service in their own right?

The study

The research with parents on which this book will mainly draw was based on a study at the Centre for Research on the Child and Family at the University of East Anglia (UEA) and funded by the Economic and Social Research Council (ESRC). There were also separately funded parallel studies at the University of Bergen, Norway (Moldestad and Skilbred 2009; Skilbred and Moldestad 2010) and the University of Gothenburg, Sweden. The findings demonstrated that across the three different child welfare systems and cultures, the experiences of parents and social workers reflected very similar dilemmas (Schofield *et al.* 2010). The fundamental dilemmas of loss and stigma that are linked to being a parent of a child who is being brought up in foster care, and the range of reactions, are shared by parents in other countries and foster care systems.

The UEA study had three elements: detailed face-to-face interviews with parents; focus groups with parents; focus groups with social workers. The interview sample consisted of 32 parents. Parents in England were recruited through three local authorities, with social workers asked to identify parents whose children had been in foster care for at least a year and were under ten when they first became fostered. These criteria were chosen so that we could track the longer-term experience of parents.

Social workers were asked to pass on details of the project to parents who fitted the criteria and parents either contacted us directly or gave permission to social workers for us to contact them, usually by telephone. Parents were given an undertaking that their participation and the study itself were fully confidential and that researchers were entirely independent of the local authorities.

As will become apparent in this book, parents expressed a very wide range of positive and negative views of their experiences as parents and of children's social work services. So although the sample may not be fully representative, we felt we had captured a fair spread of experiences and views.

The profile of the parents

The 32 parents who were interviewed had 120 children between them and 90 (75%) of the children had been looked after at some point. In many cases those children had been fostered for significant parts of their childhood, up to ten years or more. The children in foster care at the time of the interview ranged in age from 4 to 18 years, with an average age of 11. They had been aged between birth and 14 when they first entered care, with an average age of 6. So this was a particular group of children in foster care, but they were not untypical of children who have long-term foster care plans, i.e. children who come into care in early middle childhood and stay through adolescence (Schofield and Beek 2009; Schofield et al. 2000).

Sibling group size varied, but the average was four children, with several parents having had as many as six children in care. Some children who fitted our age at entry criteria had older siblings who did not come into care or came into care briefly in their teenage years and/or younger siblings who had been removed and adopted or had been born subsequently and remained with the birth parents. But all parents had the experience of separation from at least one and often more of their children in foster care.

Parents ranged in age from 29 to 55 with a mean age of 40. There were more mothers in the sample than fathers; 21 of the interviews were with mothers, 5 with fathers and 3 with both birth parents. Parents came from a mixture of rural, town and city environments. Six parents (19%) were from an ethnic minority, and two further white British parents had mixed heritage children. The majority of parents were single (17, 53%), some had found new partners (7, 22%), and four couples had stayed together despite the difficulties they had faced. Most parents were unemployed at the time of interview (26, 81%), often due to a range of physical or mental health problems, drug and alcohol difficulties.

The parents interviewed had a range of difficulties which they felt had contributed in various ways and degrees to their children becoming looked after. The most common factor experienced by the parents in this sample was drug and alcohol misuse, with over half of the 32 parents (55%, 18) describing themselves as having had problems with substance misuse. Also common was domestic violence, reported by 11 (52%) of the 21 mothers interviewed alone. Ten parents (30%) stated that they had a diagnosed mental illness, with most suffering from depression and anxiety. One parent had a diagnosis of borderline personality disorder and another had been diagnosed with schizophrenia. However, parents without a formal diagnosis also described mental health difficulties, for example depressive symptoms that became worse after their children became looked after. Four parents (12%) had learning difficulties. Four parents (12%) had spent some time in care when they were a child, and two of these believed that this was a considerable factor in their children becoming looked after. Most parents had experienced not just one difficulty, but overlapping difficulties, both before their children became looked after and more recently. It was also possible that parents may have had additional problematic issues in their life which they did not want to share with the researcher. Although statistics are not significant in a qualitative sample of this kind, it is possible to suggest that these parents had a similar range of difficulties to those reflected in much larger studies (Sinclair 2005; Sinclair *et al.* 2007).

Although the levels of difficulty experienced by parents while they were caring for their children were high, some years after children were removed not all continued to have significant personal and social problems. There was a range from parents who did continue to struggle with drugs and mental health problems through to parents who had given up drugs, met a prosocial and stable partner, gone on to have and successfully parent children and, in one case, become a supporter to other parents with drug problems. It is for this reason that the book takes a chronological route, so that the serious early difficulties and the impact of abuse and neglect on children's lives can be recognised, as well as the changes that parents went through as their lives developed. Undoubtedly for some, becoming more stable was actually possible because they no longer had the stress of caring for children at home, but many factors impact on parents' trajectories.

Interviews with parents

Parents were all interviewed in their own homes and interviews took anywhere from one to three hours. They were invited to talk about all aspects of their parenting experience, from the birth of their first child through to the present. The accounts were often very moving, as parents talked through both the highs and the lows of what life had been like for them, their partners and their children. Parents often proudly showed the researchers photographs of the children, and it was not uncommon for children's photographs, postcards, certificates, football cups and medals, achieved since they were in foster care, to be on display in their living rooms.

All interviews were tape recorded, transcribed and analysed using NVivo, a computer software system for organising qualitative data, which allows key themes to emerge and helps to identify the often very powerful quotations that are used in this book to illustrate and provide evidence for those themes.

Focus groups

In addition to these individual parent interviews, which formed the core of the project, there were two parent focus groups, to each of which four and five parents were invited, but just two and three parents attended respectively. In both groups, parents commented on how valuable it had been to meet and talk about their experiences openly with other parents. One father who had been very guarded at interview became much more open about his feelings in this setting. As with other isolated, stigmatised members of society it can be very empowering to meet others in similar circumstances. But not all parents felt able to share their views with others in this kind of forum.

An essential part of the project was to hold three social worker focus groups (one in each local authority) with a total of 22 social workers participating. These were very helpful in describing and debating the range, rewards and challenges of their work with parents.

These groups were an opportunity to put themes emerging from the interviews to parents and practitioners and to explore in discussion what parents might want and need from social workers, as well as what social workers saw as the benefits, opportunities and barriers to meeting the needs of parents in the context of their role as case responsible social workers for the children. These groups gave us some powerful insights into some of the excellent work that goes on with parents, but also into some of the difficulties and dilemmas that social work with parents presents.

Outline of the book

This book takes a chronological approach, starting with the parents' accounts of life in the family home before the children came into care; moving on to the point at which children came into care; then capturing the wide range of parents' experiences while their children were growing up in a foster family. Because contact is so important for parents and children, parents' experiences and views of contact are then explored. Specific chapters on parents' relationships with foster carers and with social workers again illustrate the range of their experiences and implications for practice. A chapter then draws on all the themes identified thus far to focus the analysis on the identity of the parents. Finally two chapters focus on social work practice: the first is a chapter on the views of social work practitioners of their work with parents and the second, and concluding chapter of the book, sets out some key issues for developing a model for social practice not only with parents, but also with children, foster carers and other professionals in the network round the child.

Throughout the book, the voices of parents will be presented through detailed quotations, which have been anonymised and with some identifying features changed. There are also direct quotations made from the social worker focus groups in the relevant chapter. The extensive use of quotations from parents gives the reader the opportunity to hear the full range of ideas and emotions and to hear how very different parents think, feel and talk about their experiences, roles and relationships. It is important to bear in mind that these are very troubling and often moving stories of separation and loss, and the picture of parents' lives that emerges does not always make easy reading. It is also difficult to hear from these accounts something of what their children may have experienced, both while at home and since being in care, the serious difficulties and the opportunities for transformation, which can be a source of pride but also of sadness for parents who could not give children the kind of care they now receive. Even where parents talk very thoughtfully about resolving some of their feelings and learning to live with the separation from their children, and even where children were seen by parents to be making excellent progress in foster care, this is not an easy situation for them to live with.

However difficult at times it is to listen to what parents have to say, the insights provided into the complexity of their experience can only help to improve social work practice. There are key tasks for parents to achieve in managing their loss and identity as parents, and these have implications for the social workers who support them during the years of their separation from their children. The aim in this book is to focus on what may be achievable in terms of good practice, based on improving our understanding of the experiences and lives of parents, as well as appreciating the complexities of the role of social workers.

2.

Parenting Before the Children Went Into Care

Parents gave very vivid accounts of becoming a parent for the first time. They described how their family lives developed, but then deteriorated to the point when the children went into care. For some parents this was a gradual process – whether steadily downhill (sometimes from the birth of the first child), occasional ups and downs (perhaps where drug use was more or less successfully managed) or as more of a roller coaster of extremes, times when perhaps being a parent had been satisfying and successful, alternating with times of crisis and threat when parents felt they were not coping and children were suffering. For most families, the children's move into care followed a long period of anxiety for them and concerns expressed by agencies. But for some, the removal of the children seemed to happen drastically suddenly and was triggered almost by a chance event. In this chapter we attempt to capture something of the complexity of each family's experiences during this period prior to care, but also the impact of a range of stresses on the parents' capacity to parent and therefore on the welfare of their children. In the next chapter we will focus on the point at which children went into care.

Although there were a number of descriptions of joy at the birth of a baby and, at times, pleasure in parenthood, parents' accounts were more commonly dominated by problems, such as drug and alcohol misuse, mental illness, family violence, loss and bereavement. Memories of their own deprived or abusive childhoods were frequently brought into these accounts, as parents attempted to make sense of why things had gone so wrong in adult life. Interacting with these stresses was quite often the size of their families. Sibling groups of four to six were not uncommon, which had implications for parenting in the period prior to care, but also had repercussions during the diverse care pathways later taken by the children, who were sometimes together and sometimes apart.

But an overarching issue for almost all families was poverty; the struggle to find the financial resources to keep body and soul together, and to provide half-decent homes and adequate care for children, interacted with other factors such as drug dependency and depression to create a sense of almost constant tension and at times despair. This was not the family life that they wanted for themselves or their children. Where violence was also an issue, the tension built into an atmosphere of fear that permeated everyone's lives and which parents reported as at times overwhelming them and harming their children. Here a range of these difficulties will be explored separately, but for many families these problems came in combination.

Memories of their own family life as children

Parents took into the experience of parenting the memories of their own parents and their own childhood. These included memories of abuse and neglect that were often unresolved, as parents looked back on their childhood with a combination of anger, regret and sadness.

> If my mother had had a bad day at work I really had to try and give her as wide a berth as possible, otherwise I would end up getting the crap kicked out of me. It was never nice – it was constantly walking on egg shells. That was when she was there. Other than that it was just me left in the house from like five in the morning until anything between six and nine at night. I had to take myself to school and that was from the age of six. I had to take myself to school, feed myself, sort myself out, bring myself home, all year round. It wasn't until I was twelve that I went into a children's home and even then it was a fight to get into the children's home. (Paula)

Parents often made links between their difficulties in adulthood and their unresolved childhood experiences. Lorraine linked her problems with mental health and alcohol to her experiences of sexual abuse.

> It is just my past, because I haven't been able to deal with my past you know. I got sexually abused when I was seven year old. I

got raped when I was eleven. I have never been able to deal with none of that.

For vulnerable adults who are under stress from these previous experiences and have developed a range of personal and interpersonal difficulties, it is important to bear in mind that pregnancy and parenthood itself are additional stresses that will have an impact on already fragile coping strategies.

Pregnancy and the early days

Although not all first or subsequent pregnancies were planned, many were. Becoming a parent was an important and valued step, for mothers and fathers.

> Everything was ready for when the baby was born. We had got everything ready, hadn't we? … I couldn't leave him alone. I used to take him out with me everywhere I went. (Jack)

The circumstances and the reactions of others to the pregnancy were not always so positive. This mother was 17 at the time of her first pregnancy and her boyfriend objected.

> I dropped the tablets I was taking down the toilet, didn't I? Because I wanted a baby… He weren't very happy about that. (Fay)

Far from being protected or supported during pregnancy, some women could also be targets of violence.

> She was planned, yes – I was very, very excited… When I found out I was pregnant I was ecstatic, but the pregnancy was very traumatic. Holly's dad wasn't exactly the most nice bloke you could meet… He beat me up, he threw me down the stairs, he starved me and I was in and out of hospital being drip fed because I couldn't keep anything down… But I knew that he wouldn't hurt Holly because he was just as excited as what I was, you know. (Gina)

As this last sentence suggests, even women who experienced extreme violence from partners separated this out from what they anticipated would be the partner's commitment to the child. It was not clear whether this belief was based on some acceptance of violence towards themselves, but it was obviously not an easy time to leave, to find housing or to face bringing up a child alone. Few mothers had good family support networks and so the need to think the best of their partner was not so surprising.

For many women, life between and during pregnancies was in a constant state of flux, punctuated by changes in partners, miscarriages and by the regular absences of partners in prison.

> I had a boyfriend I was with for six months. I found out I was pregnant with Robert, and started seeing this other bloke. Robert was six months old when I kicked this bloke out because he was violent towards me. Ray then came out of prison and I fell pregnant with Alfie, who I lost at five months. Then about two weeks after I lost Alfie, I fell pregnant with Ian and we were together for three years. I had Bradley and then I split up with Ray when Bradley was six months old. But he was in and out of prison, so it was sort of on and off for all that time. (Gemma)

Such histories were presented quite matter of factly by mothers and seemed to reflect an accepted or inevitable pattern – although it is a reminder of how complicated it is for children to track their family histories. In this case, as in others, the mother gave the sense that these were her children and that fathers, although important, would not necessarily play a major or continuous role in the life of their children. But it meant that even when they looked to partners for support, it was often without much hope or sense of entitlement.

The role of their own families

Where it was available, support from members of their own families in the early days of becoming a parent was highly valued by mothers and fathers.

> I had the support of my mum as well which was brilliant when she was around. So it was quite an experience that first time I must admit. (Jack)

But for some parents, the role played by their own parents was both intrusive and judgemental. If family relationships had been difficult before, then those difficulties spilled over into the care of the new baby.

> I think my mother took over when I had him and I think that is what caused a lot of the problems. She totally took over. I couldn't do a thing right in her eyes and we were living with her at the time. (Tina)

Because of unemployment, financial and housing problems, it was not unusual for single mothers and couples to be living with family members during the pregnancy and immediately after the birth, with varying degrees of success. But where support had been available but was suddenly lost to a couple, it could have long-lasting effects. Philip talks of their joy in the pregnancy, followed by the catastrophic effect of the death of his partner's mother.

> Yes it was great, absolutely great. I was there through the scans and all that. And then her mum died the day Caroline went into labour. It was horrible… It was terrible. I don't think she is still handling it to this day. She couldn't handle it. She don't like talking about it. Everything reminds her of her mum. If her mum was alive, they (the children) wouldn't be where they are now, she would have had a bit more help and that.

Often the loss of support in parenting children was not the only risk factor in the family situation. Both these parents were drug users, but the experience of bereavement at the time of the birth threatened Caroline's mental health and exacerbated the couple's drug use, putting this child and their subsequent children at risk.

For vulnerable parents, it was sometimes the combination of stresses in the family and multiple, conflicting sources of advice that they felt contributed to their problems. Joanne had learning difficulties, was a victim of domestic violence and lacked confidence in her ability to parent – she also knew that her daughter was affected by her anxiety.

> Amber picked up the tightness of me coping with her on my own and not knowing what is right. My mum is telling me one thing to do, my health visitor was telling me to do something, with me in the middle of it. What do I do for the right decisions? I think I made quite a few wrong decisions in my heart. I didn't have no one to look after me so a friend of mine said you have got to contact social services. Now I wish I hadn't. I wish I hadn't done that…because I would still have had her.

Memories of the children

Parents' memories of the children when they were young were often very vivid – as they are for most parents. But for these parents, such memories of a time when the family was together have become more significant and poignant as they reflect on their children's early years after the lengthy period of separation. This description was given by Barbara, the mother of Martin, now 17 years old, who came into care at the age of seven.

> Oh he was a bonny boy he was. He was a lovely little boy. Sort of blonde hair and a little bit of ginger in it – he was a lovely little boy. A dear little boy.

She has memories of good times together.

> We used to take him down on the beach and he was watching a digger on the sand at the front and we said to him once like, 'Do you want an ice cream, Martin?' and he never answered… he just sat there watching that digger go all along that beach. I can picture that now, yes.

Her memories connect the child to other family members, which was also an important way of linking the children into the whole family.

> Martin was lovely; he loved his granddad and his nanny. They used to come and see him and granddad used to pick him up and nanny and granddad bought him the buggy and all the bits, clothes and everything for him, a little bike.

Such a description reassures parents that things were not always bad and memories that add ties to their own parents were especially important.

Some of the memories were of occasions that the children had enjoyed and when they had felt like a parent. Winston did not live with his children, but used to spend time with them and cook for them.

> I remember one time I make some food, breakfast for them and well they always used to love their food and when I used to go over there in the evening to cook, I do always like a marching band and the children start marching behind me and we go in the kitchen to cook… It was just fun, it was fun, bathing them you know and putting them to bed and all that at night, it was fun.

But not all memories of the children as they got older were happy or comforting. Some parents could remember times when their children turned on them with anger because of what family life had become – in this case because both parents were heroin addicts.

> We used to have to lock Elliot out. He would stand out in the road shouting out 'My mum has got Aids, my mum's a prostitute'.
>
> **Why do you think?**
>
> That was anger, anger, and I can't blame him when I look back now. (Tina)

In a small number of cases, parents had come to blame the child's difficult behaviour for the difficulties they experienced as parents.

> She is a very active child, she was when she was born anyway, and when she was two she always wanted to have her own independence. By the time she was three that was it! She thought she was old enough to do everything, but she wasn't and that caused a lot of friction between me and her. (Joanne)

These are diverse accounts of the children – but even the more positive memories of children were accompanied by and contrasted with the stories of the difficulties that followed and led to the children coming in to care.

Drug misuse

There were many different ways in which drug misuse affected both relationships between couples and the care of their babies and older children.

It was often in pregnancy that drug taking brought parents to the attention of medical professionals. Where a mother had surprised others and herself by then being able to control her drug taking in pregnancy, it could be a source of great pride, a gift she had given to her child, evidence that she had cared enough to put the child first.

> Doctors at the time wanted to keep me on certain stabilisation drugs, but I stopped so all of my children were actually born really healthy… And now I can hold my head up and say no, I didn't abuse myself with drugs when I was pregnant. (Louise)

However, drug misuse often interacted with other difficulties. For some parents, for example, particular tragic events, such as sudden losses, appeared to have triggered problematic drug use.

> I was with Dean, you know, starting out, a flat, having a little family sort of thing and everything was OK. It was all good. We made all the preparations, you know the usual stuff you go through when you are getting ready for a little'un. The pregnancy was great, labour fantastic, you know, half an hour job done… April seemed healthy. But she went to bed one night and that was it, she just didn't wake up and she was ten weeks old. I mean obviously that then sort of threw us into absolute chaos and although I was a social drug taker before – we used to sort of dabble in a bit of everything – we weren't sort of dependent or addicted on anything, we could just take it or leave it. But after she died, me and Dean became heroin addicts and everything pretty much spiralled out of control. (Paula)

This loss of their first child, the investigation of whether they were to blame and the subsequent drug use led to the next child spending early months in foster care while assessments were undertaken. This baby was returned to Paula, but she felt that the process of separation exacerbated the difficulties she had in bonding with the new baby because of the unresolved loss of her first child. These difficulties persisted during this second child's early years and ultimately led to the child coming back into long-term care. The couple had two subsequent children who were being successfully parented. This was a sad and difficult story for the mother to tell, but for the child in foster care it may have been experienced as being singled out for rejection by her parents.

Diverse patterns of drug use and diverse family contexts led to quite varied routes to care. Although sudden downward spirals in parenting could follow rapid onset addictions, as in this previous case, other drug-dependent parents parented children for a number of years before events led to children coming in to care. Some parents talked with pride of what they had achieved in spite of their drug habits, but also with despair and regret when they remembered the impact their drug taking had had on the children. Jack and Lynn described how they managed to support each other and the six children in spite of their drug habits.

> We were both heroin addicts for fourteen years of our kids' lives right up pretty much until when they took them… (Jack)

In this family, the care of the children collapsed when the father went to prison for stealing money to support their drug habit and the mother could not cope. But Lynn still maintained that drug taking was not in itself a barrier to parenting.

> Because we were on drugs they think you can't look after your kids but you can, you know. You can still look after them kids. It is like when we used to get paid the first thing we would do is pay all the bills and get the shopping before we bought any drugs, they came last, you know we would go out and do whatever we had to do to get the drugs. But with our weekly money we would go out and pay the bills and do the shopping so that we always had food in the cupboard and the bills were always paid first… and then whatever we had left would go on drugs.

Similarly, Jenny also took some pride in her ability to parent the children while on drugs.

> I had had a social worker for a couple of years because I am a user, I am a heroin addict and my partner was also a user and the social worker used to come round once a month in case we needed any help. So bearing in mind when they were taken Timothy was sort of eight years old and I had had four kids under five, I managed quite well for eight years.

In contrast, other drug-using parents described how their need for drugs did take over and how finding time to use drugs and getting into debt to buy drugs had left the children coming second in their priorities. This was a situation in which children suffered, as Tina was very willing to admit.

> Well they were managing to go to school at first but when you are on drugs you know you say to the kids if you go to bed now and give us a break you can have tomorrow off school and so we got ourselves in quite big problems, quite quick. I would say from the start of me going on it to three months, I was probably as bad as somebody who had been on it for ten years. Using sort of five times a day.

In Tina's family, efforts were made not to use criminal activity to fund their drug habit, but the day they got their benefits, most of the money went to pay debts.

> The kids never saw anything but they were aware and like on pay day they would come home from school and I would say, 'Oh the Giro hasn't come'. Because like what we were doing was we never like stole off anyone to get drugs, but we had people we could borrow off, but you would have to pay double back. So like we might get £300 on pay day, but by the time we had counted out who we owed money to, there might be £18 left and that would be it. I mean the kids always got a meal everyday, but there weren't enough, there was never no food in the house, there was never no heat.

Tina, like other parents, described the impact of this kind of family life on their children – and in particular how they could understand why their children were angry.

> Elliot was seeing his friends getting things and he weren't getting nothing. I mean sometimes they would have to go through the dirty washing piles to find something clean enough to wear... Very angry. And I can understand why.

As well as the children's upset and anger that they could not live like other children, they often had some deep-rooted worries about their parents. Parents talked of how anxious their drug taking had made their children.

> Well you know they worried about me constantly. The only time they would think not to worry was when I was in the institution and that was actually what my son said to a professional psychologist, 'I sleep well when mum is in rehab or in prison because I am not worried about her'. So I think it had a dramatic effect on them. (Louise)

This evidence of children's concerns when they were living at home about the welfare and even survival of their parents fits with stories in later chapters of children's ongoing concern about their parents while in foster placement.

Parents who were off drugs in most cases at the time of their interviews reflected on the period before care and showed some understanding of their child's experience. It seemed likely that for some it was only now that they could let themselves think about the impact of their behaviour on the children. This mother was asked if she realised at the time how worried her children were about her.

> I don't think so. I think in my mind's eye at the time I was looking on the children as being watchdogs and burdens, because of what I wanted to do with myself. It was quite sad, you know when I look back, you know it was quite a miserable existence and totally governed and driven by my addiction. Everyone around me went through the wringer with me, because of my behaviour. (Louise)

Where parents had been aware, to whatever degree, of what their drug taking was doing to the children and felt guilty, one of the patterns that Louise and other parents described was to try to compensate the children for the impact of their drug taking.

> Ella didn't feel that she wasn't loved when she was with me. Although I was quite ill and on drugs, you know, I looked after her to the best of my ability. I told her I loved her, I tucked her in bed, you know and because of my guilt, I would be totally overbearing with external things – because of my guilt.

Some of these attempts at compensation led to criminal activity, with mothers describing how they went shop-lifting to get nice clothes for the children. But it was also apparent how some compensatory behaviour might actually lead to allegations of poor parenting by professionals, as Paula described.

> I would actually try and over compensate for it and I made a point of having to spend time with Alice – even if that meant not putting her to bed early, you know and letting her stay up really late, then I'd still get to have time with her. She didn't really have a routine or anything…routine had to sit around us instead of the other way round.

Where their care of the children was acknowledged to have deteriorated and children had gone into foster care as a result, parents still took comfort where they could. They might hang on, for example, to the fact that at least some of their children had some happy memories, even though these memories would have been mixed with others of quite significant difficulties and separations. Tina had experienced both drug and mental health problems.

> Luckily the elder ones can remember when we had a lovely house. I would clean my house. It was spotless. The little two maybe don't remember all that, but the older two do. So they knew that, apart from psychotic episodes which were normally dealt with by tablets, a couple of times I had to go in hospital, it was the drug thing that ruined everything.

Overall there is a very mixed picture of the parents' perceptions of the impact of drug use on the care of their children. There are some suggestions that parents had been able to function for periods of time. But there was also a range of descriptions of the negative impact on children, often when drug use combined with other problems, such as crime, violence and mental health problems, which meant that their children had little predictable parental care and attention and suffered as a result.

Alcohol misuse

The pattern and impact of alcohol misuse was in some respects not so very different from drug misuse, with both mothers and fathers entering cycles of drinking to excess that disrupted family life and affected their ability to be emotionally available to and care for their children. Often parents came from families who drank or families where drink and drugs were combined. Louise, whose own main problem was drug use, talked of the death of family members.

> All my family are dead from alcohol addiction, I lost my sister at Christmas because she couldn't stop drinking you know, eventually her body just stopped.

Perhaps because even excessive drinking is to some extent legal and socially acceptable, it is not so surprising to find parents who were quite heavy drinkers, but who had relatively settled histories until something happened, such as separation from a partner, which led to a downward spiral. One mother described having a business and a good standard of living, but after leaving her husband her drinking went out of control. Also significant for her was the fact that she then started a relationship with a partner who was also a heavy drinker and who therefore did not challenge her drinking. As she remembers it, the only thing they had in common was their drinking.

In a pattern similar to drug-using parents, those addicted to alcohol described how central it became in their life, in part at least because of the need to manage the physical addiction, as Amy described.

> I was keeping myself going, you know. I knew what I had got to drink and when I had got to drink it. I couldn't go more than like two hours, otherwise I would start shaking and sweating and be ill. So it is like medication really, you know you have just got to keep doing it. But then obviously as you are getting further into it, you are having to take more and more to get you to that stage.

Again, in retrospect and some years after stopping heavy drinking, Amy can recall how hard it had been for her eldest daughter to cope with her behaviour.

> It was worst for Naomi really, because she saw me when I was really, really ill and she used to beg me not to drink anymore. I used to lie to her and tell her I hadn't been drinking, but she got very clever you know. She knew from the expressions on my face. And you don't realise, you think when you are an alcoholic, you think that nobody knows, but obviously those that are really close to you do know – and she knew.

A child's fears are always likely to be fears of abandonment, but Amy can only now recognise how that must have felt to her daughter.

> Naomi was upset about it, because she knew what I was doing. She was frightened of me killing myself, that is what she was frightened of. She kept saying, 'Mum you are going to die'. But in the morning when you are vomiting and being really, really ill, that is not nice for a child to see, especially when it's your mum. But at that time you don't see it, you know.

Perhaps not surprisingly, and for similar reasons as drug-using parents, alcohol-using parents tried to compensate the child for the distress the drinking was causing. Amy described how this behaviour was linked to the need to pretend to the outside world that all was well.

> Because I think when you are an alcoholic you try more, because you are afraid of other people noticing that you are not doing things right or whatever. It is the same as cooking, I was always cooking, you know, there was always food there. I think that through the AA [Alcoholics Anonymous] and talking to other people you realise that that was all part of being an alcoholic. You know, washing

and ironing, you are always doing something… Everything had to be perfect because otherwise you subconsciously, you don't know you are doing it but you are thinking that people will notice, you know, that you are not coping.

It was a battle to maintain this façade, but behind it, for many parents, there was awareness that if the truth got out the child might be removed. This in itself became an extra source of stress to the parent and at times the child. The parents' drinking problems were a secret that children as well as parents had to keep.

As with drug use it was easy to see how children were drawn into their parents' difficulties with alcohol. The problem was not only that care was not good enough, it was also that children were witnessing, monitoring and worrying about their parents' drinking, while losing out on their education, in spite of parents' efforts to manage or compensate.

Mental health problems

Mental health problems of some kind and to some degree were common among the parents, as was to be expected from other research on parents of children in foster care (Schofield *et al.* 2000; Sinclair *et al.* 2005). Some parents had diagnoses ranging from depression to personality disorder, but others described a range of mental health and personality difficulties, especially arising from experiences of abuse and trauma, that may not have led to a formal diagnosis but had an impact on parenting. The trauma of multiple losses in their families, often in violent or distressing circumstances, was likely to have contributed to a vulnerability to depression in particular. For example, when asked about her own family, Barbara who suffered from depression and had been hospitalised said:

> I did have two brothers, but one passed away in a house fire, the other one took 56 tablets of my mum's and diabetic injections, so he took an overdose.

The pressures leading to or exacerbating mental health problems in parents had often come from their own experiences of abuse in childhood, with links made by them from their abuse to drug or alcohol misuse and to other mental health problems. Lorraine had unresolved childhood experiences of sexual abuse that contributed to excessive drinking and a range of mental health problems that affected herself and her children. But even though she had good reasons to have had problems as a parent, she saw herself as to blame for the children going into care.

> I blamed myself – I was going through that hurt. I wanted to commit suicide.

The intermittent absences that hospitalisation of a parent caused seemed to have been managed in some cases where support was available, but were likely to have left some legacy of anxiety about separation for children that added to their difficulties later.

> I have always had trouble coping with the four of them, but I have always had quite a bit of help. I have got mental health problems as well, and so occasionally I had to go into hospital when they were little and things like that. But yes, when there were all four of them, I had them within five years, I was just like normal really. We had a nice house then and yes everything went alright at first. (Tina)

Partners with mental health problems could also become difficult for the other parent to manage, as Lorraine explained.

> The children weren't happy here and I think that was due to me meeting my new partner, because he was a schizophrenic and he was going behind my back and he took an overdose when the kids were here. He was upstairs doing it. The kids were downstairs but they knew about it, they saw him get taken away in the ambulance, you know.

Lorraine was aware of how the children were expressing their feelings about what was going on at home through their bad behaviour at school. But she was also well aware of how social workers were seeing and having to make judgements about this.

> The social worker would look at how they were at school and because they were behaving badly at school, they thought, that was they knew, it was coming from home life. The children have got to show their anger and they were taking it out on one of the kids in school. We had arguments in front of the kids and they were displaying their grief and upset and anger at school.

Mental health disorders were often linked to or at least exacerbated by violence, with the combination of parental mental health problems, fear of violence and actual violence having an impact on the child's behaviour. In turn, this challenging behaviour in the child could make it impossible to cope.

> The next time it was a bit vicious – he (partner) attacked me and I sort of attacked him back and the police were called… He treated me very badly, knocked me about a bit, but I could take it and I hit back as well. Carly got stressed out – and then I got the shakes and I've got mental health problems now, an anxiety disorder it's called. Carly was picking up my stress levels and the bad behaviour started. I couldn't cope with her bad behaviour. (Joanne)

As with other difficulties that parents experienced, mental health problems were rarely the only difficulty – not only violence, but also drug and alcohol use interacted with mental health problems to play a part in a number of the more damaging family environments for children that parents described. It is apparent that a simple label or category 'parents with mental health problems' will never fully explain the parents' experience, any more than it explains the impact on the child's experience. When social workers are working with parents of children in foster care, it is important to have information about specific mental health histories, diagnoses and prognoses. But each parent's ability to move on in their own life, and in relation to their psychological capacity to offer support to the child, will be affected not only by other factors that caused and were around when children came into care, but also factors that have affected parents' lives and mental health (for better or worse) since.

Domestic violence

The experience of violence between partners, mainly (but not only) violence against mothers by fathers and other male partners, was a dominant feature in a number of families, often persisting through long-term relationships into which a number of children were born. The example given above of extreme violence in pregnancy was matched by several accounts of violence at different stages in the family's life.

Where violence from partners was concerned, the impact on women and children could be extreme. Often children became the focus or apparent 'reason' for the assaults by the violent partner; for example, when mothers like Annette were expected to control children and keep them quiet.

> He said, 'Can't you keep them quiet?' But you can't keep a baby quiet.

How do you think the violence affected the children?

> Very badly. I didn't know, but Crystal used to hide underneath her bed and everything and stand at the door, while he was shouting and he would just go ballistic, pick things up in the garden, like a table and chair, and hit the legs off, shouting 'I am going to kill somebody!'

As in this case, it was not unusual for children to have told mothers later of how frightened they had been. Mothers were inevitably often too preoccupied at the time with their own immediate physical safety to have understood the full extent of the impact on their children, but to learn later of what their children had experienced was an additional source of sadness and guilt.

The constant state of fear in such families was at least in part because the aggression and violence were unpredictable and often apparently random.

> It was awful. He used to hit me on the head and head butt me. He would just come up near a cupboard and head butt me, knock me on the head with a dustpan and brush when I was sweeping up.

Often no attempt was made to hide the violence from the children – in some cases it almost seemed as if it was designed to intimidate the children also, as Lorraine described:

> In front of the kids, he was beating me up. I mean if I did the kids tea first and then, because you always put your kids first just in case you haven't got enough, and then I would do his, his would get thrown against the wall and he would give me a hiding you know in front of the kids. He was physically and mentally abusive and from the age of fifteen I was when I first met him I had black eyes and all that lot, and then I had all four kids.

As with some other long-term relationships with numbers of children among this group of parents, this was the mother's first serious relationship and started when she was young. The more children are born, the more difficult it is to contemplate leaving. The violence and its impact is almost taken for granted, even when parents could see how children were becoming aggressive themselves. Annette described her daughter's increasing problems at school.

> She was nasty to other children. She used to kick them because he used to kick me.

Lorraine was given an ultimatum by her violent partner when she became pregnant, and she had a termination, which she said had been for the sake of her other children.

> And then I fell pregnant again and Vince said if you have this one I am leaving. Then I put the kids first. I thought they need their dad even though he is never here, but they do love him. So I had an abortion and I was sixteen weeks gone, it was a little girl. I had an abortion and he left anyway. So my kids started being offensive to me because I killed a baby. In their eyes there was no reason for me to do that. They couldn't see how I felt at that time you know so…

There are many examples of mothers feeling criticised, at the time and since, by their children as well as by partners, family members and professionals. This increased their feelings of helplessness and hopelessness, as it was impossible to do the right thing and everything seemed to become their fault.

Often the violence between couples was supposed to be a secret, not just from the children, but also from the neighbours and the community.

> They (the children) never saw the violence, but I am sure they must have heard it. They must have heard it, because you know they are in the bedroom. But one hiding was that bad that one of the children actually did see the marks.

> **And how did that make you feel as a mum when they could see that?**

> At that time basically I just told them I walked into the door. My son at that time basically wasn't daft. I think he thought there

> was obviously something going on but he never said. It is not as though I could have done anything at the time because I wasn't allowed to go out. I wasn't allowed to take the kids to school. (Alison)

Pretending to the children that nothing was wrong would have left them more confused and unable to work out the truth about what was going on. Partners who deliberately isolated the mothers from the community were also not unusual. Sometimes the threats extended directly to the children, intimidating and terrorising them.

> Every time he used to beat me up he would drag her out of bed and say right she is going into foster care. You are going in a home and all that lot. He threatened to set light to me and Nick in bed, my little son, because he was not sleeping well at the time and I slept in the room with him. I slept on the floor and Nick slept in his bed and he threatened to set light to both of us. (Heather)

The threat, made almost in passing here, of foster care was a threat both to the child and to the mother. Although threatening children with care was not mentioned specifically in many parents' interviews, the fear of children going into care was present and real for many parents.

In what is a familiar pattern from the accounts of drug-and alcohol-affected families, mothers also tried to compensate their children for the effects of living with violence.

> Yes, they could have anything they wanted, like strawberry shortcake dolls. I just felt sorry for what was going on. It doesn't buy them love or anything, but it kept them happy, stopped them thinking about the violence. (Annette)

Professionals working with children and families have become increasingly aware in recent years of the impact of violence in the family. The pervasive atmosphere of fear has an impact on women's ability to function as parents and on children's development. Many children's high levels of anxiety and extreme preoccupation with the emotional well-being and physical safety of their mother do not cease when children go into care. The memories and the current anxieties are factors that will continue to be played out in the relationships that parents have with their children and in children's ability to accept and benefit from relationships in the foster home.

Support received by parents from professional agencies

As discussed earlier, parents rarely received consistent support from their families and friends. They were asked to comment on the kind of professional support they received when they were in difficulties and whether they found it helpful or not.

Often, perhaps as might be expected, it was practical help combined with a personal relationship that had been valued.

> This family support worker really who would give us a lift to places like with doctors or hospitals and she would take us shopping and that was the start of being involved with social services.
>
> **And at that time did you find that helpful having that family support worker?**
>
> Yes I did, because I really got on well with the woman, she was called Pippa. I really got on well with her. She was a nice woman, she was a Christian and she would do anything for anyone. (Tina)

It was often hard, though, to act on the support and advice offered, because of the stress and, at times, the fear they lived under. Annette talked about how she had gone for counselling to help her cope with domestic violence from her partner, the father of her children.

> **Did counselling help you?**
>
> Yes, they just said it was an awful situation for you to be in and you deserve better and you shouldn't be in that situation, you have got to sort of sort yourself out.
>
> **And did you ever consider leaving him at that time?**
>
> Yes I sort of wanted to get out, but then I was too frightened of him to go.

This was a familiar story and for mothers paralysed by fear it was difficult to take steps that might improve the situation.

Having the right help at the right time was a problem for most families. Parents sometimes felt that help had been offered for a long time but without success – and then a final offer of help had come too late to reverse the problems.

> They worked with us for a long while, you know, and then it got to the stage when they just couldn't… They sent down a family

> worker trying to help me manage my money and put boundaries down for the children, but I think it was all just a little bit too late. (Kathy)

It seemed that sometimes there was a gap between family support services that tried to tackle particular problems and the overwhelming sense that parents had of not coping with anything.

A common story for these parents was that requests for help often did lead to some help, but also to assessments of need that in the end moved the family into a child protection arena.

> Because I actually went to social services and said, 'Look I have got problems with Ian, I need your help'. They got a home carer to come out and the home carer said, 'She needs help with Ian, because she has got severe problems with him.' And they went right OK, because Ian was so at risk they put him on the 'at risk' register. (Gemma)

For some parents, harsh as it had felt at the time, this shift from the need for help to the need for protection was not so far from the truth.

> I just told them that I needed help and then they sort of like said that I was neglecting Courtney, which I was in a way because I couldn't bond with her. (Judy)

Because parents were concerned about what might happen if they sought help, they had often tried to conceal their problems when they actually needed help.

> I was worried and I was scared because I know what social services are capable of, you know, and I made them believe that everything was OK when really it wasn't. I should have said to them no I do need help, but I was frightened to ask for help in case something went wrong, so I didn't ask. (Helen)

Although generally there was a sense of positive reactions to requests for help, there were some very negative experiences.

> Instantly talking down to you like you are scum of the earth and I think that was my first taste of how a stereotypical smack head gets treated, even though we weren't the stereotypical smack head type, you know we didn't go out robbing our friends and neighbours and breaking into houses. (Paula)

> They treated me like some alien because I don't speak English good or I am illiterate, they treat me like some alien. (Winston)

Typically, parents looked back and recognised that they had significant problems that they could not manage. In this case the mother admits ruefully that she did fit a pattern.

> Social services got involved really because of my chaotic life style with my drug addiction and you know committing petty crimes you know the usual, single mother with a huge drug habit and no support and the wrong type of boyfriends that were in prison. You know it is sad. I look back and, you know social services got involved because I wanted help, I couldn't manage. I just couldn't manage. (Louise)

But there were parents who looked back with regret and felt that if they had been able to get help at the right time they might still have had their children with them.

Conclusion

Although these areas of difficulty described here were significant, they were often overlapping with other factors affecting parents, such as learning difficulties. So mothers with learning difficulties, who also had mental health problems or were victims of violence, might be finding it even more difficult to manage their children or to seek and use help from professionals.

For all parents, there were difficult stories to tell of the many adversities that they had experienced while they were trying to care for their children, but also of the impact that they knew these difficulties with drugs, with alcohol, with violence and with a range of problems had had on their children. Parents may have been able to share some of their concerns with professionals at the time, but it seems unlikely that they could have been open when they felt their family was at risk. Parents commented that at the time they would also not have wanted to accept the full extent of the impact on their children, and it is only after some years that they were able to acknowledge how bad things had been.

Parenting before the children went into care: key messages and implications for practice with parents

- Most parents' own histories in childhood had left them with few models of good parenting to draw on and no or few experiences of being sensitively cared for that would give them the ability to sensitively care for their children. Without help, these difficulties will persist after children are in care when parents need to relate sensitively to their children at contact or are asked to be supportive of children in placement.

- Parents' experiences in adult life of drug and alcohol misuse, mental health problems, domestic violence, homelessness and poverty will often have further damaged their ability to function as adults and as parents. Again, without help, this will affect their ability to lead settled and rewarding lives once children are in foster care. This situation may lead to a continuing degree of dependence on children for support and reduce their ability to support their children.

- Parenting is itself stressful, and so increases the risk of difficulties such as drug use or mental health problems. This does mean, however, that when children are removed, stress may be relieved and some parents begin to function better. This makes assessments more complex, as some parents start to change.

- Parents' accounts also suggest that although some valued the help they received to care for their children more successfully, parents often felt too powerless and scared of losing their children to be able to ask for or accept help.

- Although parents may have some memories of their children being happy, in the main they recall them as having had very damaging early experiences, as a result of adverse circumstances, such as homelessness, but also because of neglectful or abusive care by one or both parents. It seems likely this would have been hard to discuss when children first come into care, but parents may be able to think about and work through this later and help their children to understand.

- These shared family histories will be affecting the parents, the children and the relationships between them. Thus working with parents, as well as children, to reflect on and make sense of the past could make a valuable contribution to their ability to move on. Life story work with children is seen as a necessary step to creating a coherent story that accurately reflects their lives to date and to resolving their feelings. There may well be scope for similar work with some, though not all, parents, that enables them to gain insight and resolve some of the unresolved feelings about this period in their lives and the lives of their children (see Chapter 9 on social workers' perspectives on work with parents).

3

Parents' Experience of Their Children Going Into Care

The process by which their children went into care was always a very significant part of the parents' story. Their memory and view of what was often a very difficult, even traumatic, event was likely to have an impact on how parents viewed their subsequent parenting roles and experiences during the years that their children were growing up in foster care. It is a time when social workers are closely involved with children and their families and need to understand what this process is like for parents, in particular the diversity of their experience, in order to think about how best each parent can be helped to cope with it.

Parents' perception of the process of separation, as reported some years after the event, is linked very strongly to some key themes – in particular the difficult question of who was responsible for the children coming into care and where the blame should lie. These perceptions were likely to go on to influence the parents' self-concept and self-esteem as well as their relationships with social workers, foster carers and indeed the children themselves.

Although understanding why children go into care relies on an understanding of the kinds of troubled family histories presented in the previous chapter, the question of what actually 'caused' the children to go into care at a particular point in time, or triggered the turning point events that led to the separation, was very important in parents' accounts. The attribution of blame by parents, to themselves or to others, was very significant and yet was rarely a simple thing. It will become clear that whether the *primary* focus of blame is oneself or a partner or social services, this was usually in interaction with other factors. For those who blamed themselves, for example, their traumatic childhood histories, violent current partners or lack of support could be taken into account as parents reflected on responsibility for what happened. Similarly, most of those parents who were angry with social services or social workers recognised that their care of the children at the time was not as good as they would have liked it to be or as good as the children needed. Very few parents stated that the case for the removal of the children was entirely without foundation.

Significant in terms of parents' future attitudes and ability to work with social workers and carers is their acceptance of the need for care at that point in time. But the experience of 'acceptance', like the attribution of 'blame', may vary over time. This is a complex psychological arena, and this chapter will attempt to capture the range of different experiences and attitudes to this crisis through which parents and their children passed. In later chapters we will look at how some of these feelings evolved over the years of children being in foster care, including having to accept how much better some children were developing in foster care. But here the focus is on that initial period of loss, as children went into foster care, cases went through court, and then parents faced the aftermath, as they realised that their children were not coming home.

Blame and responsibility

Perhaps inevitably a very personal sense of blame or responsibility, and (for some) guilt, was felt particularly by parents who had been using drugs or alcohol at the time their children went into care. For them, the memory that there were times when they might perhaps have changed the outcome by coming off drugs or alcohol, but were not able to do so, was a source of great regret – although even where there was regret, many saw their addiction as being like an illness, of which they too were a victim.

Where parents were addicted to drugs at the time the children went into care, they tended to blame themselves. They often had memories of feeling under too much pressure in other aspects of their life for them to be able to give up. For some, the drugs simply took over. Tina's partner used drugs to some degree, but once she started using drugs herself, first speed and then heroin, she very rapidly became addicted.

> If I had never gone on drugs and even if he was still dabbling, I could have controlled that. But when I went on it, all control went out of the window.

Tina's son Elliot, the eldest of her four children, asked to come into care and subsequently Tina agreed that all the children should come into care.

> Elliot was saying 'I want to go in care' because he knew what was going on – he was going without and they were going without. They were getting neglected because of all what we were doing, you know, and he started saying to social workers, 'I want to go in care' – so they took him.

The sense of drug addiction being her fault and incompatible with parenting was clearly expressed by Tina.

> It's ruined my life and I paid a hard price. But it's my own fault. All through my twenties I was so against drugs and what made me change I don't know, I really don't know... I mean I have spoke to other addicts and I can honestly say no one on heroin can look after children even if they think they can they can't and no child should be left with a heroin addict parent, because at the end of the day the only thing that comes first is your next fix.

Although Tina's account names her own escalating drug use as the key trigger for the rapid deterioration in the care of the children, her husband's drug use also increased at that time. In addition, Tina had a history of post-natal depression and other mental health problems that had required hospitalisation, and the children had, during crisis times, moved between father and mother. This combination of difficulties had an impact on her children such that she and her husband were able to recognise, even at the time, that there was a need for the children to be in care and that they were not able to look after them properly.

The feelings expressed by parents in these circumstances often combined sadness with a sense that from the point of view of their children's welfare, the right move had been made. Where the children were able to reflect this perception back to their parents this was a bonus, as it suggested that at some level parents had been forgiven and were seen by the children as being good parents rather than bad parents, for at least accepting the need for care. Again, this was Tina's experience.

> Even though it was our own faults, when the little two went I was really sad. But I felt like well they are going to somewhere where they are going to be looked after... I mean all the kids say that we done the right thing, it would have been crueller to keep them here.

It helped Tina when she reflected on this period that she had anticipated that better care would be provided for her children and had found that to be the case. Her husband, Derek, expressed similar feelings of sadness and guilt, and agreed that going into care at that point was necessary for the children. He built this sense of having done the right thing into his advice for other parents.

> I have whole nights where guilt keeps me awake and I just think of my kids. But yeah my advice to other parents is you have just got to hold your head up high and get over it, not get over but get on with it... If you are making that child suffer by living at home, by going hungry and saying it is my right to keep social services away, I think that is wrong. I think if you are in a position like me and Tina were in, the best thing we should have done is put the children up.

Their shared acceptance as parents of the need for the children to go into care has almost certainly helped them since to remain a close couple, who supported each other in staying off drugs and in maintaining the best relationship with their children that could be achieved through continuing to show their commitment and through contact.

There was often a sense of inevitability as downward spirals of drug taking and crime became out of control.

> There was always food in the fridge, that kind of thing, but it was really hard work to keep up. I was doing petty crimes, you know shop-lifting kids clothes and stuff like that. I wasn't sticking to the scripts because I didn't like methadone, so I'd score some heroin. You know it was really sad actually, eventually there was no stability for my children. You can't be in an environment where you [the] sole carer is getting arrested, going to prison, you get accommodated and then get given back and then after a little while the same cycle again, deeper and deeper. (Louise)

Sometimes the sense of personal blame for drug-using parents was tempered by the fact that the situation was beyond their control; for example, Lynette reported how it felt when her husband and father of their six children went to jail.

> Well he ended up getting four years in jail and I was left by myself with six kids and a heroin habit and I just couldn't cope. I ended up, you know, in the corner with a blanket over my head, 'Go away, leave me alone'.

In this case, although some responsibility was accepted by this couple, the nature of drug addiction (including the fact that you may get caught up in crime to pay for it) meant that the risk to the children, as they saw it, was not entirely their fault. Fathers in prison when their children go into care seemed able to minimise their role and distance themselves to some degree from responsibility. As Lynette's husband Jack put it:

> It's a case of they have taken the kids away because they felt they would be better off yes. Because ours was nothing to do with abuse or neglect or anything like that. It was mainly because of her breakdown and me being in jail that this all happened.

This father had eventually asked for the children to go into care. While in jail, he was asked to think about whether the children were safe at home with his wife.

> Well they basically said to me you know, 'We are worried about the kids…what do you think we should do?' and I said, 'Well you know it is a bit of a hard thing to be asking me when I am sitting here in the jail'. But it had actually come to the stage where I was getting sort of stories coming in from other people and through social services telling me how much of a mess she had got herself into. And it actually got to the stage where I had to put my hands up and say to social services, 'Go and take them', literally, 'Just go and take them'.

Jack tells this story in terms of being a good father at this point, showing concern for his children and taking a difficult step. Although he dissociates himself from the possibility of abuse and neglect, he did express regrets about getting sent to prison and his failure as a father to keep the family together. He initially came across as defiant about his capacity to parent while on drugs. But when asked about whether he looked back to his own childhood for role models as a father, he talked of his own family experiences before he himself went into care and how much in fact he regretted his involvement with drugs in adult life and the impact on his family.

> I was arrested when I was fourteen for attempted murder on my stepfather. You know he made my life hell. He really did make my life hell. So no, I don't look back at that at all.
>
> **Do you think you have been a better father than he was to you?**
>
> No, no, to be really honest, I don't. If I had been a better father I would have been there a lot more, do you know what I mean? I wouldn't have gone to jail. I wouldn't have made such a damn mess of things, which I feel I have done in the long run. Even though for fourteen years I felt like I was doing really well and people have said to me like 'I am surprised you coped that long' but when I look back at it now I shouldn't have been involved in that damn situation in the first place especially having kids around. It is a sickness, it really is, it is a disease and once it gets hold of you there is no letting go, there really isn't.

Such a complex mix of emotions and sense of regret and failure featured strongly in parents' accounts of many different circumstances. Mothers in relationships with violent or verbally abusive partners, in particular, often felt a similar combination of anger, blame and regret that they had not made different choices. They expressed anger at their partners for the harm done to their children and blamed them for the loss of the children that resulted. But they also expressed regret and anger at themselves for not separating from their partners earlier and not protecting their children, thus accepting some degree of blame.

Mothers reported living through often extended periods of violence and then reaching turning points that led to the children having to go into care. These turning points were when it seemed that children were affected in more extreme ways, not only by neglectful care, but also by witnessing violence. Children were described as starting to fear for their own safety, but also, in some cases, appearing to model their behaviour on the violent partner and becoming violent themselves.

> They have seen him hit me and thought they were going to get it as well… The children were bullies because they were seeing what they saw at home… I mean my oldest boy he has gone out and beaten people up, he has got five GBHs [grievous bodily

> harm] and his dad thinks it's funny. He says, 'Go on hit him, hit him, hit him with the dog lead...' Malcolm started displaying problems. Like when he went to school, he started being a bully and he put some little boy in hospital. (Lorraine)

Often in these situations it was when children started school and outside agencies became aware of the difficulties of mothers and children that families dominated by violence came to the attention of children's services.

Where mothers recalled being too preoccupied with managing the difficult and violent relationship with their partner to care for the children, the sense of regret and the wish that they had their time again were profound.

> I blamed myself. I weren't there for my kids emotionally, you know. If I was then they would be here now, you know. If I could turn back the clock you know I would do it. (Lorraine)

> I didn't think he had a drinking problem but he had, you know. It just went wrong; wrong partner, wrong time, done the wrong thing, chose the wrong person and that was it. I still blame myself. (Joanne)

Some parents felt that they had not realised at the time what they know now about children needing protection from harm. They expressed regrets which they linked to advice for other parents.

> Just think what is best for the children really you know. You don't want them to be hanging about in families who are drinkers or drugees and things, because it does reflect on the children, I realise that now. I mean I wished I had got out of that relationship ten, fifteen years ago. I think if I did get out of it earlier things would have been a whole lot different you know, things would have been more stable and secure and things like that, you know. (Karen)

Even when a partner was not violent, a new relationship could lead to couples getting more deeply into drugs or alcohol so that children became more neglected, again leading to a point where children went into care.

> I met some bloke and then everything just went downhill. You know they were still getting fed, but that was like emotional neglect that

they went through. Because I was drinking and I weren't there for them as much as I was when I was a full time mum on my own. (Lorraine)

Very often the parents' accounts gave powerful insights into what life had been like for parents and children and why they reached the point of accepting, however regretfully, the need for care. Mental health problems often combined with violence and it was possible to see how children had been moved from one disastrous situation to another, as mothers tried to find some kind of stability. During the period that Kathy had her first five children, she had several partners and, whether on her own or in a relationship, suffered significantly from anxiety and depression. On her own she could not cope, and her downward spiral followed a relationship with a partner who bullied her and culminated when she was moving from place to place, hostel to chalet, and although social services intervened to offer some support, she simply could not cope. Kathy was only too well aware that her children were not getting the 'normal childhood' she wanted for them.

> I agreed with them because I knew that whatever happened the kids needed and deserved regular meals, clean clothes, a warm bed you know and even though they hated it at the time they needed school, friends that they could bring back you know, just a normal childhood.

But Kathy was able to take comfort from her continuing love for the children, while recognising that at the time she could not care for them.

> Whatever happened I didn't mean it to turn out like that – irresponsible parent I am not. I still loved them, they were still my kids and I would still do anything for them if I could do it, just in a rather unconventional way. I have to say it again, I have never stopped loving them and I never will, they are my kids you know. I was just a crap mother.

Kathy was a particularly reflective parent, who had worked hard to make sense of and come to terms with the loss, but also to do her best to support the children and work with foster carers over the years of their placements.

Although their inability to separate from a partner was described by a number of mothers as the primary reason for the children going into care, it was possible for some mothers to put this in the context of their own traumatic history. For Lorraine, this connection between her own abusive childhood and her adult life helped her to some extent to resolve some of her sense of responsibility and self-blame.

> I have never been able to deal with none of that. I got physically and mentally abused by their father in the first eleven years I was with him for you know. It is just hard and that just all come back and you know I couldn't, I had to deal with myself and my kids and that just got on top of me and I couldn't do it. So that was when social services went in there, they were right there. And they were picking up on every bad thing that I done and that is what made it worse.

For this mother, the involvement of social workers left her feeling further persecuted rather than helped, although she recognised that her own difficulties were significant.

Where mothers reported feeling too frightened to separate from their partners, these situations were rarely simple. Because the risk of breaking up the family was also such a concern, levels of violence could drag on, with neither the mother nor professional agencies taking a decisive step. Then even after years of concern and attempts to manage the situation, children in these families might come into care permanently after a particular incident or, for example, because the mother decided to give her partner one more chance. Annette explained her decision to breach a court injunction and take her children to see their father during court proceedings, because the child asked to see him.

> Caitlin cried every night and I couldn't do nothing with her. She was saying, 'It is my dad, how dare you stop me from seeing him?' And she had quite a strong bond with him. And I thought, you know, it is not doing them any good and I thought well for her to be taken into care, you don't think that a spur of the moment mistake, which is a really bad mistake, can lead to it.

Very often court proceedings will be a period when the family is closely assessed or even tested and a line is finally drawn. But for Annette, her feelings about her partner's responsibility for the circumstances that led to the children coming into care and her own acceptance of some responsibility were mixed with anger at social workers and a sense that she had not really been a bad mother.

> I thought what gives them the right really? Because I hadn't really been a bad mother. It was only because of all the violence and everything that I got punished for it. I was a good mum though, I never hit them or done them any harm. But they didn't see it like that. They said I wasn't protecting them which is why I failed I think.

From Annette's account the violence not only towards herself but also the children was extreme. But her explanation for the admission to care includes recognition of the seriousness of the harm and her own failure to protect them, while still suggesting that somehow the social workers had 'punished' her by removing the children.

For other parents too, although some responsibility was acknowledged, the degree to which they were deemed by social workers to be at fault was challenged. Louise described how leaving her children in the house while she went to get drugs had led to allegations of neglect.

> I went out to score while my children were in bed and I got arrested. So naturally I am in the police station, my children are on their own, I had to tell the police that my children were on their own, even though I didn't want to. You know my plan was, you know it sounds a bit mental now, was to run out, get what I needed, which would usually take ten to fifteen minutes and come back. But that night I got arrested and that is when involvement started in a big way, because it was neglect. And my argument was at the time, no it isn't, my parents used to leave me when I was ten to look after my sister. And you know, I just wasn't listening, I was just frightened.

A description of their parenting as 'neglect' at the time the children came into care was often disputed, mainly because the term was taken to mean something else, but also because their current living circumstances were not seen as any different from their own childhood. Louise felt like this.

> Well I don't think I thought they were wrong, but I didn't understand what they meant by neglect. You know my idea at the time of

neglect was pretty much children getting beaten and starved, you know, and I know today the dangers, which if I am honest was the way I was conditioned as a child. It seemed pretty normal, that kind of situation.

More complicated, but not uncommon, were the circumstances in which a concern about the children that had brought the family to the attention of the police or social services was not directly the parent's fault. However, the resultant investigation had raised concerns about other aspects of the parent's care of the children, and it was those subsequent concerns that led to permanent separation of the children into foster care. One example of this type of case was where parents had trusted friends or family members to look after children temporarily, but the children had then been harmed. In Gemma's case, once the investigation had taken place of bruising to her children while in the care of a friend, other concerns were raised about her parenting. This situation was complicated by the behavioural difficulties of her sons, one of whom was later diagnosed as having ADHD (attention deficit hyperactivity disorder).

> They said the reason they are in care is because they suffered physical abuse from an adult and I went yeah fair enough, I have explained all that. They said, 'But you couldn't cope with them'. I said, 'I have been telling you from day one that I couldn't cope with Ian, but you just said it is the way I brought them up.'

Such cases show how judgements about blame and responsibility for harm to children are not simple and rely on an overall assessment that children are not thriving and are developmentally at risk in their parents' care.

Also difficult to manage are situations where a child may come into care abruptly, for example when parents are arrested and imprisoned for offences unconnected to their parenting.

> We got arrested and we got charged with others, so Natalie came to the police station with me until 6 o'clock at night. They said that children weren't allowed to be in the police station after 6 o'clock, so they were getting social services to come and collect Natalie. (Amy)

In this situation feelings of responsibility for the separation that arose from the imprisonment were quite distinct from feelings of blame as a parent, although Amy had previously had problems with alcohol and described herself as having been an alcoholic.

Entirely my partner's fault

The parents discussed thus far may have varied in their sense of whether it was right or necessary for children to go into care, but all recognised that there were problems in their care of the children and to a greater or lesser extent they accepted some personal responsibility for that. There were parents, though, who entirely blamed their partners.

Heather and Steve who had long been separated at the time of their (separate) interviews blamed each other, telling stories of very extreme behaviour by their partners. Having this opportunity to hear both sides was a reminder of how difficult it is for social workers to sort out what really went on in terms of the 'truth' and what might be thought of as their responsibility for children being in care. But it was also a reminder of how for their children in foster care it must be almost impossible to distinguish between these completely opposing views of their childhood and to fit either version consistently with their own memories.

A rather different situation was that of Darren, who had been caring for his daughter, Daisy, prior to the child's final reception into long-term care. He attributed the damage to the child's development that led to this separation to the previous care by her mother, who had significant mental health problems. Darren had separated from his partner prior to the birth of their daughter, and realised over the years that her mental health problems were putting the welfare and safety of their daughter at risk. After one of a number of short admissions to care, the child was returned.

> It wasn't long before social services again had to be called in. Her mother tried to commit suicide by walking along the train line. She was sectioned into a mental hospital; the kids were taken off her.

When Darren agreed to offer Daisy a home, he learned more of what she had been through. However Daisy's behaviour continued to be a serious problem for him and his new young family – not helped, as he described it, by contact with her mother. Eventually Daisy went into foster care long-term. Although Darren blamed his ex-wife for the harm to their daughter, he nevertheless also appeared angry with Daisy and seemed to suggest that he and his wife had done their best for her and she had not responded to their attempts to offer a home as she should have done. This was one of a number of cases where disputes between parents and older children trying to fit into second families were mentioned as problems that contributed to the need for long-term foster care.

Social services and social workers are to blame

Parents' accounts of the role of social workers in the process of the child or children coming into care were often complicated and related at times to the general organisational responsibility of social services. There was, for example, the context of what social services did and did not do in terms of support, child protection interventions and court. For some parents the feeling that social workers and this large organisation were to blame had much to do with an overall sense of being powerless and a victim.

But although social workers represented social services, and indeed 'the authorities' in a wider sense, they were experienced by parents in many cases as acting as individuals, and parents quite often referred to the role of specific social workers. Where social workers were blamed for the children coming into care, it was not unusual for this to be described as an act of personal vindictiveness, as this mother describes:

> She hated me from day one. Whenever she sees me in the street she tries to talk to me and I will not talk to her.

Although many parents had mixed views about the role of social workers, some were fixed in a state of anger. For Peter and Fay, it had been abuse caused by someone asked to look after the children briefly that began the process by which the children came into care. However, there were concerns that then surfaced about the parents' own care of the children.

> The reason why they got taken into care is because I got heavy on the drink. I was getting to be an alcoholic and I asked the social services to put them with my brother until I sorted myself out and

then my brother apparently hit the kids and then I found out then
that they were in care. (Peter)

Both Peter and Fay have maintained a very angry stance over the years,
although they could comment on at least one social worker who they
liked and could get on with. Peter also suggested that one particular
social worker did not like him, but then said that this was because he
had threatened the social worker, saying, 'If you take my kids then I
will smash your face in. I will throw you off that balcony.'

Drug-using parents varied as to how they felt social workers had
judged or misjudged them. Parents who defended their ability to care
for their children while on drugs felt that, as Jenny describes, social
workers did not understand and so judged them unfairly.

> There was that one time when they come round and I had had
> a bit of crack and it didn't make me paranoid or whatever, but
> obviously I was more aware. And they just said, 'She just seems
> to be all over the place', as if I didn't know what I was doing. And
> it wasn't that, it was just more me being nervous because I had
> had some gear and then they come like knocking on the door...
> Loads of people use, they can't work every day but they manage
> their kids fine, they manage their house fine and all that. But as
> I say at the end of the day, they made it worse for me, I feel my
> children lost out, I have lost out.

Jenny's account is full of references to health visitors, neighbours and
other social workers who she said agreed with her that the children
should not have gone into care. She primarily bases her case on the
fact that her children were not abused in the way other people's
children are. Rather like the mothers quoted above who disputed the
definition of neglect, Jenny disputed the threshold at which it was
right to remove children.

> My kids should be with their parents unless, do you know what
> I mean, they are being battered, sexually abused and all that...
> Help them as much as you can if they need help from outside,
> but take kids off parents as a last resort. It makes me sick knowing
> there are kids being found dead in flats and all that because the
> social worker has gone to the door and not got an answer for five
> months and they ain't bothered do you know what I mean?

Jenny's memory of family life suggests that there were problems, but she did not accept the need for care.

> My kids they were doing fine, they were doing well at home. My kids didn't need to be taken off me and as much as I am a user and alright yes there might be some things they missed out on, but they certainly wasn't unloved do you know what I mean? They were clean and tidy, they enjoyed Christmas and they enjoyed their birthdays, we went out and done family things and all that. If anything with presents and money sometimes we might have over compensated through being a bit guilty through using, but they still got the love and all that they needed you know.

This account brings together both Jenny's challenge to the criteria used by social workers and courts and the sense that her children were loved and, in the main, looked after. One of the parent focus groups for this study was held at a time when the newspapers were full of reports of the death of a baby known to health, police and social services. These parents too reflected on how much worse such cases were than their own and saw this as a justification for doubting the judgement of professionals in their own cases – and as reassuring them that they had not been so bad as parents. The gap between their own view of their situation and their sense of the standards by which they had been judged was very clear.

But, significantly, many accounts from even the most angry parents showed how attitudes to social work decisions, like acceptance of their own responsibility, might change over time. Gina's account of events combined a range of angry statements about social workers, and yet over the years she had changed her view of her family life with the children at the time they came into care.

> Hectic, the house was dirty, the children were dirty, they said, and two had head lice which are a nightmare to get rid of… And then I didn't agree with them taking them, but now I do.

Again, it seems not so straightforward to classify people, for example, into those who are angry or hostile and those who are accepting of the need for care, when change over time is taken into consideration.

Supposed to be a short break

It was not an uncommon experience for parents to have agreed with social workers to children coming into care in a crisis but expected that children would be returned when the crisis was over. Then the children remained in care.

> I was angry because they said that I needed a break. I said yes OK I need the break… I thought OK two weeks that is fine I can get back to normal and get back into a routine. And when the two weeks was up they said no they are going to stay in care further and I went why? Because, they said, we don't think you can cope very well. (Gemma)

Gemma's two children who were taken into care at that point had been in foster care for ten years at the time of the study. Although angry as she remembered this process, she now thought that this was the right thing for the boys, as they have thrived in spite of their difficulties.

> At the time I was disappointed and upset they went into care. But looking back I think because I had so many kids so young that it was best that Robert and Ian went into care because they did have their problems.

Other parents reported that they may have accepted that there was a problem requiring children to be looked after in foster care, but said that they had not expected it to last.

> Social Services were coming round and they came round one day and made this pact that if I put them into voluntary care and got myself sorted out, I could have them back. Well here we are, five years, six years down the line and I haven't. They came in the morning, they came back in the afternoon. They didn't even really give me a chance to say goodbye.

In a number of these cases it was possible to imagine how assessments might have led to social work recommendations and court decisions that it was in children's best interests to remain in care. But it is also important to recognise where parents felt the process moved too fast, did not respect their feelings or did not seem honest.

> My only qualm with social services is that they shouldn't have lied to me and said that it would be easy for me to have them back when you sort yourself out because it is not. They don't tell you that and I swear they still don't tell people that to this day. (Kathy)

There were parents who had been very unclear as to what 'foster care' meant when their children were first taken into care for a break. Claudette had come from the Caribbean and did not remember getting a proper explanation from the social workers of where the children were going when she was admitted to hospital for psychiatric treatment. For her, though, it was the later realisation that this separation was permanent that was the source of anger and distress.

> She and another woman came here and took them and they didn't mention foster care, because I don't know what foster care is all about. I have never been there and my children have never been there. I had been looking after my children up to the age of eleven so they had never been through that before and I don't know what it was all about. I thought they were going to a centre or some place where money is and they could play and have fun with other kids, until I come home and then I get them back. But I didn't realise that it was somewhere permanent. So it was hard for me because I was very tearful, I was crying. I was in real distress because I wanted them back. I fight to get them back. I went to Court three years ago to fight to get them back and the Judge said that I could see them four times a year and speak to them once a month.

The reason given to court for the permanent separation in foster care also stayed in her mind, so Claudette's fight to get the children back over the years was also about proving that she was not a bad mother.

> The social worker said that I neglected and abused them. And I said that I may neglect them, but I don't think I abused them. And she said to me that they should stay where they are. I said but why? I am on medication because I am not well and I am doing well on my medication, I see my CPN [community psychiatric nurse] every week, so why can't I get my children back. Why can other mothers have theirs and I can't have my mine?

In contrast, there were some parents whose children had been in and out of various kinds of short-break or respite care prior to the final separation, but were returned to parents each time. Louise, who misused drugs, described how, far from welcoming the quick return of her children or their removal from the child protection register, she felt unready to cope and missed the support.

> There were respite periods where the children were accommodated in care while I went to therapy. And I would come out and the children would be returned a bit too quickly, if I am honest, or taken off the 'at risk' register – which pissed me off because I wasn't getting the help. I felt somewhat, I went into this artificial environment, came out with a certificate and you know looking healthy naturally because I hadn't been using, I had been eating and all that stuff. And then the children would be returned, the door would be shut, I wouldn't have a social worker any more, I had to be referred to Duty which I didn't want to because I was scared of the power.

For non-resident parents, there was also a sense that repeated and quick returns had not been helpful, as Darren described:

> They were taken in. They were in and out of emergency care about two, three times a week. Each time she (mother) got them back, once or twice I said, 'Do you think that is really a wise idea?' but again social services, 'Yes, yes well they belong with their mother, the mother needs to have her kids with her'. And that is what I got each time. Although fair enough I wasn't in a position to do anything about it, because I was living by myself in a bed-sit.

Voluntary relinquishment

Some parents had reached the point where they did request or agree that the child be taken into care. Joanne had started drinking heavily and was also in a violent relationship that had an impact on her mental health.

> Yes I rung social services myself, because I was shaking, I was literally shaking. I couldn't even hold her, she was quite young then. She was only two and a half. You imagine a two and half year old. I was in the kitchen, they do run behind you and I am shaking like a leaf, I couldn't control my legs, couldn't control my arms, couldn't control my tremors. I was so scared that I could accidentally scald her and I couldn't stand the thought of her being in harm's way. It was for her own safety at the time.

But not all parents felt that they had made the decision freely.

> They were going to get took anyway, so I jumped before I was pushed… It has made it sound a little bit better to say like well 'I put my kids in care' than to say, 'My kids were taken'. Maybe that is why I done it as well, because it sounded better you know. (Tina)

For this parent it seemed preferable for the children to feel that the parents had made the choice for the sake of the children; for others it was important that the children knew that parents had fought for them. Such differences in how the coming into care process was understood affect the messages given to children and affect how parents view care, view social workers and also define themselves as parents.

For most parents, the process of children being voluntarily admitted to care was often preceded by social workers expressing concern. At times the situation appeared to leave parents little choice. Kathy remembered agreeing to the need for care, yet at the same time feeling under some duress.

> They came round, I think it was an arranged visit, I can't remember. And she said, 'I just think that now you really need to think about your children you know', and I could see her point. And she tried, I can't explain, I can't remember everything. But the fact was that if I arranged for them to go into care voluntarily…because they made it quite clear that if I didn't they were going to go through the, is it the courts or the Police? to do it. Because they felt that the children needed it now.

For Claudette, the experience of losing previous children who had then done well in foster care meant that her new-born infant was relinquished before the end of the mother and baby assessment. Claudette had significant mental health problems, having been treated for depression and schizophrenia. Her decision was made to protect the new baby from the negative experiences of her older siblings.

> In the end I stopped it [the assessment], because I said I want her to stay with the rest of my children, because I don't want her to go through the same thing that my other children went through when I had them, when they were going to school, because when they were going to school they were abused and harassed by other kids and I didn't like it.

In this case, the mother was able to choose for the baby to join three older siblings who were in the care of a foster carer whom the mother trusted. At the time of the interview, this mother was expecting her fifth child for whom the plan was to go straight to the same foster carers, to be adopted by them.

The day the children went into care

As these accounts indicate, although there is diversity of experiences and views on the reasons for children going into care and the process, all parents had to manage the experience of loss and find ways of explaining it to other people and to themselves. But important for all parents were their memories of the day the children went into care.

When the decision is made that children need to go into care for their own welfare and safety, there will be a day when that separation occurs. However necessary the separation, and whoever made the decision, this will be a very difficult day to face – for parents, for children and also for social workers. Given these descriptions of families reaching a crisis, parents on drugs, children not being fed, violence and the inevitable trauma of separating or being separated from your child, the day the children went into care was a difficult story to tell.

Some parents had the experience of an infant being removed from hospital days after the birth.

> It was very tough, because it was very upsetting. They took Carly from the hospital with two of the foster parents and she was getting uptight because the social worker didn't know how to deal with her and she was getting stressed out. I was getting stressed and anxious myself and it was really bad, she was really crying her eyes out. Because she was only ten days old, she didn't know what was going on. When we got to the house she got settled in and the foster parents said I could stay for about half an hour, so I stayed there with them and when I walked away I just got home and shut myself in at home and I just cried my eyes out for about a week, shut myself off from everybody. I went into myself. (Joanne)

Painful as this account was, the stories of what this day was like for older, school-age children and their parents were particularly graphic accounts – not only of the parents' distress, but also of the distress of the children. Dolores described her children's reaction and her own anger.

> Wednesday morning I took them to school and when I went to pick them up two social workers were there with Keisha and Joel. Oh, we are taking them into care. And I can tell you that was the worst day of my life because Keisha and Joel they didn't want to go. They started crying for their mum and the thing is because I was in shock I said if I had a gun I would have shot them, I would have shot them social workers, I would have killed them.

Even when we know that the children had been at considerable risk, these accounts cannot fail to be moving, as they combine the ordinary everyday actions for parents, such as picking the children up from school, with seeing them being driven away to live with other parents, foster parents.

> Russell went in the afternoon and they let me pick the other two up from school – and as soon as they were home from school they took them too…
>
> **How was that for you?**
>
> Horrible. (Heather)

Sometimes the process had felt too rushed, and parents said that they had not had time to say good-bye.

> **Describe that day to me, what was it like?**
>
> Heart wrenching, there ain't no words to describe it. You just curl up in a ball. Despite what had happened I loved them and I didn't want to be without them. (Kathy)

Where the removal of the children was planned, there may be less shock, but it can create very difficult periods of waiting for the separation to happen. Gina and her partner were told on the Friday that their four children would go into care on the Monday when placements were ready. They say they were asked not to talk to the children about it over the weekend as the children would get upset. Then on the Monday one of the children in particular became very distressed and refused to get in the car.

> Holly said 'I am not going to go because mummy doesn't want me to go, do you mummy?' And I said, 'No, I don't want you to

go' and the social worker was saying that I was being, what was the word they used to use, I weren't 'co-operating'.

Gina believed that it would have been worse for her subsequent relationship with her daughter if she had said that she wanted her to go if that was not true.

There is no easy way to move children, particularly older children, into foster care. There were few children who had experienced deliberate harm from their mothers: most cases combined emotional and physical neglect, with some children having witnessed or experiencing physical abuse from their father or their mother's partner. Although the evidence of significant harm may rightly be persuasive to professionals and courts of the need for care and protection, for the children themselves that particular day will be like any other day in their lives – so this begs the question for the child, 'Why do I need to leave now?' It is also not uncommon for older children to have come across the idea of 'care', but most often used as a threat or held up as a terrible fate. When it happens to you, it is not surprising that children are desperately anxious about what it might mean, and parents' perceptions of 'care' will often not be very different.

Court and afterwards

Not all cases went to court (a minority of children remained accommodated on a voluntary basis), but for those parents who had this experience it added another layer of anxiety, stress and helplessness. Even the idea of 'court', with its associations with criminality, was hard to bear.

> That was very hard, that was very hard, very hard for me. It affected me very badly, because I have never done a criminal offence. I have always stayed on the right side of the tracks… I got very upset about it, didn't have no one to turn to. (Gina)

Parents felt surrounded by powerful people involved in their 'case', with those on their side outnumbered by the rest.

> If you have never been through court proceedings it is very hard for somebody. You are on your own with a solicitor, then all social services, their solicitor, it can be very daunting, plus the Judge. It can be a very, very daunting thing. (Joanne)

Even where parents felt at the time or subsequently that the right decisions were made by the court, they resented being 'found guilty' and they would have liked more of a 'defence'.

> Yeah I still feel guilty as sin. I am not critical of the decisions, but if I burgled your house or mugged you I would have got a defence. I was guilty as charged without a defence. (Joanne)

What was particularly galling to some parents was that so many cards had seemed unfairly stacked against them at court. Helen described how her former partners, who were fathers to her older children, appeared with their solicitors and watched her struggle to defend her care of their children. These partners had been violent or shown little interest in the children, but were presenting themselves as concerned fathers. She had also decided she should just tell the truth to assessing psychiatrists and the court. But by the time she had described in detail her very difficult childhood, her problems with partners and drugs – and become very distressed in the witness box – she said the consensus was that she was a very damaged person who could not care for her children, given that history. Helen seemed to accept that the outcome was right for the children, but nevertheless felt that she had suffered for being open and telling the truth.

For many parents, including Helen, the feeling that they could not win the case was overwhelming, so it was a matter of damage limitation, primarily with the goal of maintaining as much of a role as a parent as was possible. Helen, for example, had contact with her older children in foster care and was grateful to have at least some contact with her younger children, who were adopted by their foster carer.

Kathy decided not to continue opposing care proceedings if her daughter could stay with her foster carer and she could have contact. But she also had a new, more stable partner, was pregnant and needed to commit herself to establishing her new family.

> I dropped out of the court proceedings in the end because I knew I wasn't going to get her back. Right, I said, I am not going to oppose it any more. I underwent all the assessment, the psychologist, psychiatrist and all that... I said if she had contact but stayed with Bridget, I would drop it because I was fighting a losing battle. I was pregnant with Finlay and I sort of had to come to a decision that most mothers would hate to have to do. I had

> to drop one for the sake of the other. But it was a case of, it is really hard, this unborn baby. When they said Olivia wasn't going to be adopted, she was staying with Bridget (carer) and I could have the contact, I had to take a step back and think long and hard what I had to do. And I decided in her best interests, not mine, she should stay where she was, but be a part of my life as much as she can.

Maintaining some role and parental identity in relation to the children following the court case was always going to be key. But, again in terms of damage limitation, other parents talked not only of the significance of the opportunities for contact discussed at court, but also of the times when they felt that judges had been on their side in putting the record straight about them as parents. For example, one father was pleased that a judge had struck out references to allegations of sexual abuse from the court record because of lack of evidence. When parents are aware that they have failed or even that they have been publicly deemed to have failed, and are losing so much, these points in time when they felt fairly judged or that important people were on their side, and redeeming features were noted and valued, were remembered as key parts of their story.

But however anxious and isolated parents had felt during court processes, they often felt even worse afterwards. During care proceedings parents were involved in a whirl of activity: visits from social workers and guardians, visits to psychiatrists and solicitors, appointments at the clinic for drug tests, often frequent contact with their children until the decision was made.

> I couldn't plan anything because I was going to court, I was seeing the social workers twice a week, I was going to the other people twice a week, I was going to see a psychologist, I was going to see you know all different people so they put labels on me, they would tell me what kind of person I was. (Helen)

Parents needed a diary or calendar to keep track of it all. Until decisions were made, however stressful the process, there was always activity and a glimmer of hope. But once the order was made, the attention of professionals turned away from the parents. Even the social worker who still had a role with the parents focussed on securing the child's placement. Contact often reduced, if not immediately, then over time.

If a child moved from a short-term to a long-term foster placement, carers would be unfamiliar and the carers' commitment to permanence (promoted by social workers) may have appeared to exclude the birth parents even further. These are all issues to be taken up in later chapters, but it was notable that this area of practice was one on which parents and social workers agreed – parents would experience a sharp drop in the attention paid to them and the support available for them once court was over and the plan for the child to remain in care throughout childhood had been made.

> I have been on my own ever since. No one has been, no-one at all. I think you do need support even if it is once every two months, you know, just someone to talk to. (Joanne)

Then, finally, after court and the decisions had been made there were the reactions of the world to face. However much it was possible for them to see themselves as a parent who had tried to do the right thing, the point when the children went into care could be very hard to manage among family, friends and community. One stage in their lives as parents was over and the next was beginning – learning to live as parents of children who would be spending their childhood not with them but with their foster families, and whose lives they would only ever be able to see in glimpses.

Children going into care: key messages and implications for practice with parents

- However long running and serious were some parents' problems in caring for the children, there was usually a trigger event, either in the family or the professional system, that led to the children coming into care. In some cases, there was an accumulation of problems well known to children's services that came to a head when concerns became more serious. But in other circumstances, a relatively minor event, once investigated, revealed family problems that had not been known to children's services. These different routes could lead to different kinds of difficulties in coming to terms with the process, in particular the balance of anger, sadness, blame and responsibility.

- Questions of blame and responsibility for children coming into care are key to how parents experience and remember this time, and the emotions that are then associated with it, such as anger, guilt or relief. Many factors will contribute to parents' appraisal of their own role in these events. These factors may relate to their own previous family histories, the actual role of violent partners, the nature of the professional interventions and parents' general capacity to face up to stress and personal responsibility.

- However, the parents' appraisal of their role and the role of others (partners, their own parents and professionals) may change over time, just as their emotions may change. Talking to parents at a point in time, as researchers do but also as practitioners do, can only capture the history as seen through the parents' eyes at that point in their lives. This is valuable, but it is important to bear in mind that the person met now may have changed from the person who was judged to have harmed the children. Both the past and the present need to be understood, not only by case-responsible social workers, but also others, such as Independent Reviewing Officers who manage the review process.

- The experience of loss and separation is a dominant theme, with memories of events, such as the day of the separation, being very vivid and poignant.

- Changes in identity and self-esteem in the context of loss and stigma were important factors in how parents described the separation. But they were complex, with parents offering often apparently contradictory appraisals of who was to blame and the impact this had on their self-esteem and identity as parents.

- The experience of court was often a defining moment, in terms of feelings of powerlessness, shame, isolation and being an object of criticism. Feelings of abandonment after the court order had been made were also common. Although parents were often angry at social workers, some felt the loss of someone who had been with them throughout the proceedings, while others may have preferred a new social worker.

4.

Parents' Experience of Their Children Growing Up in Foster Care

The move of children away from the family home and into foster care, even in circumstances where the move was accepted by some parents as necessary, was an event that for most parents caused subsequent grief reactions similar to that of a bereavement. Shock, denial, anger and depression could last for months and even years, with only some parents able to reach some form of resolution. The loss is experienced at both a private and a public level, with the personal loss of role and relationships being compounded by the stigma attached to losing children to the care of the state amidst allegations of neglect and abuse. Even their entitlement to grieve for the loss of their children may not be recognised, because of the blame that attaches to parents through the court process – hence the concept of 'disenfranchised grief' (Doka 1989).

For many of the parents, by the time of the interview there had been a long journey as they tried to find ways to manage their loss and their lives as parents of children in foster care. In this chapter we look at how parents describe the early days, their first reactions to the loss of their children, and then explore their often changing perceptions as their children were growing up in foster families. But it is important to remember that for many parents, it was their feelings of regret and grief that were hardest to manage, and which underlay both positive and negative views of having children in care. Kathy described her feelings of grief and loss.

> Awful. The hardest thing really is the grief. They are alive, they are
> healthy and they are safe – but you have still lost them.

But she also realised that she had to live with the responsibility,
however hard.

> I don't pretend to forgive myself, right. I just have to try and
> understand how they feel. With the boys, even to this day I find it
> hard. But you have to accept that I made a mistake and I have
> to live with it.

For parents who accepted that their children needed to go into care,
the fact that, over time, they did well went some way to changing the
intensity of the grief and the feelings of guilt.

> I still feel guilty, but not quite as guilty as I used to when I first done
> it. I am glad I did, because they are getting on so well you know
> (crying). (Karen)

So running through this chapter on the parents' views of their children
being in foster care are their longer-term perspectives on their children's
progress, as well as the shifts and (for some) progress in their own
lives as they adjusted to the implications of having children in care.
Throughout was the necessity of managing their changed parental
identity in the context of stigma, which could mean they were treated
like a different person.

> Well it was horrible, because when your kids go, people look
> at you differently. People talk to you differently and you get the
> people, the 'there is no smoke without fire' brigade. The people
> who think well they must have done something, you know even
> worse than being on drugs and it is just horrible, the stigma
> attached to parents whose kids are in care. (Tina)

Managing the loss

Loss affected the parents and had to be managed both immediately after
the children went into care and in the longer term. Like a bereavement,
the impact on parents of the loss of their children could be physical as
well as psychological.

> As soon as the boys went that night, I didn't eat. I couldn't eat for
> three days. (Chantelle)

For some parents the overwhelming feeling at that point was that they had lost everything and were in fact no longer parents.

> I wanted to do myself in because life weren't worth living. I didn't have nowhere to live… I didn't have my kids. I didn't feel like a mum. (Lorraine)

The psychological vulnerabilities that led to their failure to cope as parents often contributed to a downward spiral that followed the separation. Lynette had mental health and drug problems, both of which got worse after her children were removed.

> I ended up having a nervous breakdown and after they took the kids well I just went on self-destruct for two years you know. Oh I just cried, cried me eyes out, and then, I just went out and got myself a load of gear [heroin], just done all that and just got out of my nut to try and forget about it, you know.

The downward spiral after children went into care was particularly extreme for this mother and she described herself as 'running away' and 'putting her head in the sand'. During these two years she had no contact with her children.

The combination of past and present difficulties led to problems in managing the feelings of distress at the process of separation. For Lorraine, who had been abused as a child as well as experiencing violent relationships in adult life, her conclusion was that she was just not 'worthy' to be a mum.

> I did see myself as not worthy to be a mum, when they first got taken, because I blamed myself and I weren't worthy. I weren't, you know, good enough to be a mum.

After the children went into care, the intensity of her sense of loss was exacerbated by all the other losses she had experienced, but left her questioning her identity as a mother.

For parents who go downhill initially after the children go into care, it is hard to lose this sense of desperation.

> I didn't want to go home because it was like a graveyard without the kids and I was just very vulnerable, I wanted to obliterate myself. (Louise)

For two years Louise was more than once at risk of death from drugs, but once she had reached rock bottom she took stock, moved to a different area, recovered from her addiction, and went on to become a support worker for women with addiction problems.

Jack, away in prison at the time that the children went into care, described his feelings as a father that had to be put on hold in order to survive.

> I was absolutely smashed to pieces to be honest, but the trouble is when you are doing a sentence in jail you can't allow your head to be out here otherwise you don't survive. So I just literally had to swallow everything and shelve it and deal with it day by day. I had twenty-four months of that.

Early contact after the children went into care provoked strong feelings and could also be hard to manage. Some parents could not bear to see their children for contact.

> At first I was so choked up that I didn't like seeing them after that, when they first went into care. I didn't see them for about five weeks, six weeks after that. (Steve)

Sometimes in the early weeks, older children were too angry and upset to see their parents. Lorraine's son ran away from care in the early days and then did not want to see her.

> When they finally found Malcolm he didn't want to come and see me. He did hate me; he blamed me for him getting taken into care. The other three did come and see me, but they were upset, they were crying and that was just bad contacts, because all of them were crying and thinking about why they were in care.

Although for some parents a downward spiral followed the loss of their children, for others, there was a certain kind of relief. The children were being looked after safely and 'care' was not as bad as some parents feared, especially when they realised they could still see their children and even have some role in their lives.

> I still have a say so in their lives. I didn't know until someone phoned me up, I think it was one of Zak's carers at the time, can he have a haircut? They take them away and that is it really, it is not explained. (Kathy)

Once the children were no longer their responsibility, the pressure was off and some parents were able to come off or control their drug and alcohol use. Tina and Derek said with some pride, but also ruefully, that they had come off drugs a matter of months after the children went and have remained off drugs since. Helen also talked of how she became determined to show everyone that she could come off drugs and turn her life around. Her two youngest had been adopted, but she still had a teenage son in foster care who she felt needed her and saw her as 'mum'.

How difficult or bearable the early days were depended to quite a large extent on how parents felt the children were treated by the carers, how contact with the children was managed and how they were treated as parents.

> Irene treated them really nice. She had fun with them and she would get them all things, decent food. She got them to eat more things than I did actually. They wouldn't eat a lot of vegetables, but she got them to eat vegetables and they had a healthy diet. They had nice clothes and she would take them out on Saturday down the beach and she would do loads with them.

> **Did the foster carer treat you like their mum?**

> Yes she would say how they were getting on and you have been their mum and everything, she never ever doubted me, she always made me feel welcome. (Annette)

But for all parents, in the longer term, their lives and roles as parents were dramatically changed by the absence of their children. As after other kinds of losses, what should have been family occasions were always difficult, for fathers and mothers.

> It is not the same. It is like I don't celebrate Christmas because they are not here. (Peter)

> Christmas, that is the worst time for people with children in care, that is the worst time, it is Christmas. To think that you are not with them, Christmas day. You are not opening their presents, seeing their little faces. You are not playing with them on Christmas day. (Joanne)

Christmas and birthdays may not have been the perfect occasions when the family were together, but special occasions for families are nevertheless particularly poignant reminders for parents who are apart from their children.

For parents who did not have other relationships or a supportive family, it was especially hard to get on with their lives after they had lost their children, as Claudette explained.

> I don't have no family here. I have family here, but they are not there for me and I am on my own, so my children are what I need, my children are my family. That is why I miss them. That is why I miss all of them and that is why I want them back… I wanted a big family of my own and that is the reason why I have children and I love children. Yes I miss my kids deeply, but what can I say? They are happy where they are now so I just have to live with it and accept it, I have no choice.

For Claudette, although she is clearly angry and upset by the loss of her children and talks of wanting them back, there is still an acceptance that they are happy in their placement – though this thought is not without its own pain.

Preoccupation with the children

Linked to managing the sense of loss was the challenge for parents of managing the emotions, often the anxiety, that they felt about the children. Accepting the separation was especially hard for parents who were very preoccupied with how their children were getting on in care. Parents felt left out when there was no easy communication. Annette remained preoccupied.

> I think about the girls every day. Wondering if they are well, how are they, what are they doing, if they are happy, is everything alright… I can't get in contact by picking up a phone to say how are you? I feel really left out of it all.

Even when they knew that the children were probably fine, parents might worry, as Annette did, especially at certain times of day.

> I know that is all OK, but I just worry what they are doing, you know at home and when it is bedtime I think, oh I hope they are not worrying about anything, that is just a thing you get I think, instinct I think isn't it?

Living with these worries could get better over time, but parents like Annette had to find ways to manage their emotions and cope.

> I do get upset a lot about it, but then I hide it all and put my brave face on. Whereas before I couldn't cope and I thought 'I am fed up and can't be bothered to do anything', now I make myself do it.

As will be discussed in more detail in later chapters, the potential for more open communication and regular information from foster carers and from social workers seemed to be important, even when children were expected to be settling in the foster home and becoming part of the new family. But it was apparent that knowing how the children were doing was important in helping parents to feel less anxious and to experience some sense of continuity as a parent.

Perceptions of children thriving in foster care

What kept many parents going and helped even the most regretful and angry parents to become more reconciled to their children being in care was where they perceived that their children were thriving over time – and where parents felt that they were still their sons and daughters to love and be proud of.

One of the most encouraging aspects of the stories that emerged was the number of children who were seen by parents as having thrived in care – and also the number of parents who were able to enjoy and appreciate this progress.

> Olivia is happy. She is settled, she is bubbly. She has got a better social life than we have. She goes to Brownies, After School Clubs, Summer Holiday Clubs, oh God! She is having a field day! (Kathy)

> It is a little village where they live and he is really happy there. Ian has got two foster brothers and two foster sisters and he is really happy. He is doing his exams at the moment. (Gemma)

> Russell has settled down really good…he is brilliant now. He is much better compared to where he was, because when his mother had him, she used to leave him in a buggy all day long, and now if I see him in town with the carer, he is always walking everywhere. (Steve)

Several children had been difficult and troubled children to care for at home and the knowledge that foster carers were helping them to do well was reassuring. For some parents, it was the child's recovery from problems arising from abuse that was especially pleasing

> I am really proud of Paul, really proud. I mean he hated swimming. He hated water because of what his step mum did to him – she nearly drowned him in a bath of water. And I am glad he loves swimming you know and I am really chuffed that he plays football. He is a proper little boy. (Judy)

Most parents realised, as Judy did, that their children had not been easy to care for and they were even more proud of the child's subsequent achievements as a result.

> When Paul first went there, they had a few hiccups, but now he is doing really, really well and I am proud of him. He does gymkhana, he does horse riding, and he does all sorts of things.

Progress was sometimes attributed by parents to better financial resources, although they were also able to describe effective parenting.

> They are really, really good with Robert as well, because you need someone with a firm hand. He has just turned sixteen, so now it is sort of 'You must still do your homework' and 'You must knuckle down' and he is a typical boy. (Gemma)

Where children had been parented in ways that helped them to thrive in spite of their problems, it was especially valued that the parent had not been excluded from some degree of involvement. Gemma felt very much included in Robert's life through regular phone calls with him and his carers.

Louise praised the carers who worked to help her daughter, Grace, to be happy, but saw her regular contact as helping Grace to answer the question, 'Who am I?'

> My youngest child is in a fantastic placement. She is a very happy child, she is getting on well. She has got a few problems as most of the children do in care. You know if they grow up, they want to know who they are. But I have had consistent contact.

It was impressive that some of the placements had been stable for many years, so that the parents as well as the child had only needed to get to grips with one set of relationships. Parents realised the value of this stability and also the opportunities it brought.

> Robert moved into Gloria and Andy's and he has been there ever since. He has been there ten years now and he is doing really well.

> **What do you think has helped him to change?**

> Knowing that he is allowed to stay with them full time. Knowing that he is allowed to go to army cadets.

In this particular case, the mother, Gemma, felt that she and the carers had had to fight to get permission for her son to join the cadets, and that her support for the carers on behalf of her son showed how she could make a difference, even from a distance. It was satisfying for her to know that not all the credit for winning this battle went to the foster carers and that her son saw that she worked with the carers to make things better for him.

Parents' appreciation of what carers have done for children was often in the context of foster families with very different lifestyles, but as long as they cared for the child and passed the test of being 'down to earth' in their relationship with the parents then the situation could be accepted and even valued.

> Well I don't know how you would describe them; because they are sort of um…where they actually live the foster dad is a potter. He has just built his own pottery. They have got a massive great… I suppose it is meant to be an orchard out the back. They have got ducks, they have got chickens, they have got dogs, they have got cats, they are all like into the organic. They are vegetarians. They allowed Robert to eat sausages when he first got there, but now he is into eating more vegetarian stuff. But they are really, really nice actually, I get on really well with them. They are down to earth. (Gemma)

This story illustrated the way in which a child can be incorporated into a very different family and lifestyle and thrive. Gemma appreciated not just the material changes, but also the fact that her son received the kind of firm controls she could never give him.

> They are relaxed with Robert, but they are always strict as well. They always make him do his room. They always make sure he comes home. They won't let him watch telly until he has done his homework. He is only allowed two hours of PlayStation. He is not allowed on the computer without asking them first because they have said they have got to put the parental control on, which is fair enough. I am pleased they do that. But they are really, really good with him, they are really good with him.

Where children had been in a less successful previous placement, even parents who may generally have been very angry at social services were genuinely pleased when new carers seem to be helping their child to fulfil their potential. Barbara's son had a learning disability and attended special school. She and her partner expressed anger about the fact that her son was in care, but they appreciated a good foster carer and were keen for her son to live as full a life as possible.

> Mother: We find the placement with Graham (foster carer) is a real breath of fresh air, because he is allowing Martin to do things now that the other foster carers simply wouldn't allow… He is now allowed to get on a bus on his own.
>
> Partner: We couldn't want a better foster carer.

Where children were with good carers, this made life more comfortable for the whole family, and parents could relax too.

> I mean the whole relationship has been, you know, so it goes smoothly for everybody. With my two youngest children, social services managed to get some funding to get them the kind of homes from a private sector they thought they needed, the kind of carers they think they needed to suit their ethnic backgrounds and their emotional needs. And you know I have got to say that went very well. (Louise)

Louise's children had been in care for seven years and she appreciated that social services had gone the extra mile to make sure that the needs of these two children were met.

The contrast with the kinds of lives that could have been offered to children in their birth family were often graphic, particularly the opportunity for holidays abroad.

The only thing I get asked about is if he is allowed to go on holiday. I had to sign a bit of paper saying that Jim and Vera can take him away. That did happen when he first went there, but now he just goes tripping off.

When you were asked to sign that piece of paper how did you feel?

I didn't want to sign it – but then I think well it gives him that experience that I didn't have when I was a child so he can go away places. (Sophie)

Parents who had either asked for children to come into care, or agreed that this was necessary, found a range of ways to reassure themselves that they had made the right decision. They were able to compare, in particular, how the children had benefited from foster care with what might have happened if they had stayed with them. Key to their sense of themselves as parents was that this decision was part of a continuous process of loving them and that often they themselves had been victims.

I made the right decision for my kids because they were put into placements where they would be constantly looked after twenty four seven. They have got my love. I have always loved them. But I was still a kid myself. I never had, you know, I wanted children because I wanted to be loved and feel loved. But I was a good mother up until I met my ex partner and then I got ill treated emotionally and mentally you know ill treated by the ex so…

What do you think would have happened if the children hadn't gone into care?

I don't know, I suppose they would have still been here. But I think because of them being in care they are more settled, they are more happy in themselves, they are doing well at school, which they weren't before and they are happier now. (Lorraine)

Permanence

As most of these examples show, the parents were at varying stages in accepting the role of carers as parents and the child's need to belong to the foster family – an issue that will also be discussed in later chapters. But for some parents there was an appreciation of the total commitment of carers and the way in which the carers had come to love the child and the child had become part of the foster family.

> But this woman Kelvin went to, she was getting quite old and was giving up fostering, but she decided to make him her last one and he is still there (five years later). He is doing an 'A' level course at college. He is doing really well now. He is going in the Navy… This lady is seventy, but she doesn't look it. She has got more energy than I have! He is like their world; they absolutely dote on him and he wants for nothing. She actually specialises in special needs kids and she is so good. He absolutely adores her you know. It would destroy Kelvin if he had to leave her. (Tina)

This mother and her husband were highly accepting of the fact that their children were in care as a result of their former drug misuse. They supported each other in believing that it had been right for the children to go into care, valued the involvement they could have though contact – and, alongside their ongoing sadness, were genuinely able to feel love and pride in their children and appreciation of the carers.

In a number of cases, full acceptance of the child's place in the foster family was not seen as ruling the child out from a full place in the birth family. Where there was regular contact the parent experienced the child as having two families – and, in this example, described the child as being and feeling lucky.

> I always see Olivia on her birthday or just after. Christmas is the same. I am forty next month and I am having her on my birthday, so we can have the rest of her extended family down, my parents and that, to celebrate. Everyone came down in May just after her birthday, because she was here for the weekend and we threw a big tea party, so she had two parties.
> So Olivia sees herself as a lucky little girl. She has got Bridget (carer) and Bridget's family that love her to bits, and they do, and she has all the normal things, parties, treats and then she has mummy and Owen and the boys, her brothers and she has another family. She is loved so much that little girl, she couldn't want for more.

Parents who fully accepted the care situation made it clear that they accepted all that went with this, including the carers and the child having a life over which they as parents had no control. But this apparent relinquishment of control could be positively framed, as with Gemma who saw herself as having given her permission to the foster carers and to her son to be a family.

> Whenever I phone the carers up and I say to them, look are you going on holiday this year, they said well we are thinking about going to such and such. I never say to them no you can't go, I just say to them look Robert is in foster care – wherever you go on holiday it's up to you. I said to Robert if you go on holiday all I ask is you let me know when you get back, OK, and he went OK.

One of the key questions about permanence in foster care is the range of decisions that carers or parents can make (Schofield and Ward *et al.* 2008). Parents sometimes had to make decisions that weighed the children's best interests in the foster family against the child's role in the birth family.

> **Do you, when carers ask you about things like holidays or haircuts, do you ever say no to anything?**
>
> I am pretty easy going about things like that. There was a party for my brother-in-law's fortieth and my nephew's thirteenth and with them being close my brother in law obviously wanted Lily and Jacob to be there. But I thought about it and it didn't take me long to make a decision, because I wouldn't want them missing out on going on holiday for ten days to Spain just for the sake of one night of coming to a family party you know. (Karen)

Parents were often aware that children themselves might feel awkward talking about what they enjoyed doing with the foster carers. So it was important for parents to give children permission to enjoy what the foster family had to offer.

> I think sometimes with children in foster care they feel guilty to tell you they are doing this or they are doing that. But now they know that I haven't got a problem, well they have always known I haven't got a problem with the foster parents, they are sort of, 'Oh mum, Bruce done this for me' or 'Gwen done this for me'. (Tina)

This state of acceptance was rarely there from the beginning, but more commonly grew over time. Parents had often felt in the early days the need to assert their rights as parents and to challenge the carers' right to care for the children. But over the years, this attitude shifted when parents became less angry and preoccupied about their loss and could appreciate what good carers could offer their children.

> You know there have been times when I have phoned up and said, 'You can't do this to Julian', and 'You can't talk to him like that' – but we have moved on from that. It is now three years, so we have gone past that bit and they are just doing their job at the end of the day. It was me being uptight thinking, that's my child, how dare you! Do you know what I mean? But, yeah, great people. (Helen)

Even where parents would have liked to have children home, they could understand the benefit of the longer-term plan for the child in foster care.

> **Does she still want to live here with you?**
>
> Yes she would, but I don't want to disrupt her. She is doing well at school, she goes up to big school in September you know and she can have a better education and life and which is good so… (Karen)

In these situations parents felt themselves to be making painful choices that would not be what they or maybe the child wanted, but would be in the child's best interests. It may be that a court would not have allowed the child to return home anyway, but for a parent to accept the long-term plan of foster care meant giving up the fight for, or at least the hope for, the child's early return. This meant being asked to make a choice that put the child first and themselves second, and thus required a generosity that many found hard to maintain when they were themselves lonely and wanted to have the child with them.

> **And how do the carers treat Adrian? Do they treat him well?**
>
> Yes he is part of the family. He has a key to the house. They take him on holiday, you know. They discipline him when he needs it. They push him when he needs it. He is quite happy there. I should think they treat him well.
>
> **Are you happy to see or to know that he feels part of their family? How do you feel about that?**
>
> Well, I do have stuff around that obviously, and you know sometimes I am OK with it and sometimes I just feel a little bit inadequate… But I have to stay positive. (Dolores)

Mixed feelings are inevitable for parents who have to live with the fact that their child is happy living in another family.

Parents' concerns about children in foster care

Inevitably, not all children were so lucky in their pathways in foster care as in the cases just discussed, and parents talked with a combination of anger and concern about children who had, for example, experienced multiple placements because their behaviour made them beyond control.

> Callum is up in double figures at least. They have moved him about so much it is unbelievable. Because he was getting in so much trouble the foster parents just didn't want to know after a couple of weeks, do you know what I mean? He was ruthless weren't he? Violence and all sorts – he was getting right out of hand. But it got to the stage where people wouldn't take him in you know. (Jack)

In contrast, some parents were concerned because children were moved from places where they were settled to places that could be permanent. Where things had been going so well, it was frustrating for parents if children had to move because carers could not offer long-enough care. They worried for the children.

> The woman that had Alistair, her name was Iris, his foster carer and she was lovely. I actually asked if she could adopt him, but because of her circumstances unfortunately no. That really did make me angry because like he was from me to her and then from her to somebody else. It is going to mess his head up. (Judy)

But it could be hardest when parents had concerns about whether children were being looked after properly and wanted them to be moved. Some parents reported very negative experiences that children had in certain foster families. But as this experience showed, where the foster family is not able to meet a particular child's needs, moves in foster care can be necessary and beneficial – and appreciated by parents.

> Well they were together with a woman and she was nasty to them. And Adele kept running away and she ran away five times in two days, but they kept taking her back. I mean she was literally running from this house in the middle of the night with bare feet, walking miles to get to like friends of mine's houses or back here. When she came back here we just had to get the police to come and take her back again. Then social services found her this new place where she has been ever since and she has been really happy. (Tina)

Where children were getting into trouble while in foster care, parents could see that events that care was supposed to prevent were unfolding nevertheless. This led parents to suggest that the children might as well be at home with them – and might even do better.

> They can't deal with the two kids and they want to come home, they hate it now. Like my daughter, she is mixing with some kids up at the school, I mean she is getting in trouble with the police and that because she is stoned with this girl and nicking.
>
> **How does that make you feel when you hear that?**
>
> It really winds me up because at the end of the day she could have done it here, but I could have prevented that. She is the one that is going to be in trouble with the police all the time, I have always said that. And she is in foster care and that is what she is doing. (Heather)

Where parents have genuine concerns about children's experiences in placement, these should be listened to as not all foster carers will turn out to be good carers. Because parents may be assumed to be critical of carers without good reason, it can be particularly frustrating for them to see that their children are unhappy but not to be able to do anything about it. Louise accepted the need for care, but still acted as a concerned parent/expert on the children's needs and had clear views about what carers need to take into account when caring for children.

> Well to be honest I am just glad they are away from that particular placement because I knew it wasn't going to last. I said to Sally (social worker) I don't like this placement and I don't like my children being treated like robots and I just felt it was too clinical... I think the carers probably could have done with some training. I think their idea of being foster carers and the reality of it was two different things. Because you know especially if children have been uprooted and passed around, you know they are going to be a bit frightened, they are going to be a bit ambivalent; they are going to be a bit guarded and mistrusting.

Of the parents we spoke to, all, even the most angry about the care situation seemed able to appreciate the difference between placements where their children were happy and where they were not. Although parents will not always be right in their judgement of a placement, they may be spotting genuine difficulties and their perceptions and concerns should at least be checked.

Anticipating leaving care

Whether children had thrived in foster care or had difficulties, the question of what might happen when they reached the age of 'leaving care' could be quite challenging. Most parents (and their children) lived with the view that children were legally in care till 18, with some idea among parents that they would get the children back then, if not before. But for those parents with children well settled in foster care, there was a tension therefore, as the children moved through the teenage years, between this half-expected outcome and their own realistic assessment of the situation. This assessment often suggested that the child's progress might be better maintained by remaining in the foster family. But this question was also bound up with parents' notion of what the young people themselves might want to do.

> I don't think they will come back to me soon, because Ian has said 'I want to stay with them when I am at college, but when I am older I will be able to come home and see you' and I went 'Yes that is fine'. Robert has decided he is staying there until he is at least 25, until he has finished college. (Gemma)

Important to Gemma was the fact that the carers were willing to accept the child living with them, and used the carer's own child as a comparison.

> The foster carer said you are welcome to stay here. I mean, their oldest daughter has come back home after being to college. They said if you want to go and live with your mum, no problems. If you want to stay here and go to college no problems, they said, we will support you whatever. Which I think is good, because usually foster carers say at the age of eighteen that is it, we don't get paid for you no more. But while he is in full time education they still get paid for him so yes.

There may be aspects of the foster family life that were said to be the attraction.

> He wants to work with animals and they own a farm so I think he will end up staying there and helping out with the pigs. They have got two pot bellied pigs, you know, but he really enjoys it there.

Gemma was relaxed about her sons' choices, perhaps because she felt fully involved in their lives, they had stayed in contact with her, she had a close relationship with the foster carers, and she had a younger child at home and a stable partner – so she had a new and fulfilling life of her own.

Perhaps not surprisingly, not all parents were as relaxed as this mother was about the strength of the children's relationship with the foster family as they became teenagers. This could be a source of concern rather than something to be valued.

> It is at the back of my mind that Carly might decide when she is fourteen, fifteen, sixteen, that she don't want to see me anymore, now she has got a new family. She is probably more settled there and she can make her own decisions, what she wants to do with her life and I might not take part in it. (Joanne)

Other parents were torn between wanting their children to come home and being concerned that not only would the children risk losing what had been built up in terms of education and a positive lifestyle in the foster home, but that coming back to the area where the mother or father still lived would put the child at risk of harm.

> I want to have them back, but I am frightened of having them back in case they get in with the wrong crowd and you know end up in trouble and things, because obviously you can't lock them up and keep them indoors and watch what they are doing all the time. (Karen)

In this account it is possible to see the parent's worried preoccupation, as the arguments go back and forth in her mind. Helen was demanding to be moved nearer to her son (with whom she had a close relationship, but also on whom she seemed to rely) so that if her son did return to her it would be in a safer area.

> Julian is living with Ivy and Anthony, who are really nice people, lovely people. He keeps saying he wants to come back when he is sixteen and a half. He can come home, but they are saying they are going to keep him until he is eighteen… I have gone to Social Services pleading, if you want Julian to do well as I do, then you will try and help me get out of here. I don't want to be in London, I really, really don't. I want to go wherever Julian is.

For some parents, concerns about children returning were more specific; they were anxious that older siblings might influence them, in particular older children who were not in foster care and were engaging in anti-social behaviour.

> Social workers assured me that Thelma and Des are really good foster carers and they would sort him out. They were concerned I think as well because Brett (older son) being how he is, they didn't want Conrad to go out with him and get into trouble as well, so they wanted to get him away from the situation I think. (Karen)

This risk of negative influences from siblings was an issue for contact too (see next chapter) and it certainly raised concerns for parents when they were thinking about the child's future in care or at home.

For some parents it was unclear if they had any realistic expectation that children would return, but they behaved as if they did, preparing themselves for that day.

> I have to keep myself going do you know what I mean? I want to because I want them to come home one day and see what a good person I am, that I am not the person that I was when they were taken, do you know what I mean? (Helen)

> Just like writing to them, that is all I can do really and keep myself going for when they get older, look after the house. I take time off work you know to get it sorted and that because they wouldn't like it in a mess. (Annette)

In Annette's mind she has an idea that the children are waiting to return home, and anticipates their arrival. But it often seemed that both teenagers and parents were keeping this idea or dream of being together eventually alive, as a way of reinforcing their relationship. But they then needed to find ways of justifying the child continuing in foster care and not returning home (e.g. the constraints of the care order, etc.) because both young people and parents knew that returning home might interrupt the young person's progress and not actually work well for either of them.

But the dream of the children eventually returning home nevertheless had a great deal invested in it by some parents, in terms of compensating themselves and the children for what had been missed.

> I would like to take them on holiday and do different things, and have a nice time as a mum with them, make up for their lost years really. It is hard, but life is ahead and you can be there for when they would like to come back to you. (Annette)

When children do come home from care

Having discussed the way in which parents were anticipating children 'leaving care' and coming home or staying on with foster carers, it is also important to consider that a number of the parents had older sons and daughters who *had* returned home from care in the teenage years. This was for a number of reasons, but perhaps paradoxically was sometimes because the child was proving difficult to manage in foster care, and maybe had started offending so that other placements could not be found.

Parents reported that these young people often brought with them from foster care expectations and a standard of living that could not be maintained.

> When they all get put in foster care they have all got big lovely fancy posh houses, they have all got a car. And he sort of gets took out of that and put back here where we live on eighteen pounds a week and he sees all his friends in nice houses and he is like, mum, why can't you get a new carpet? (Tina)

Parents were not entitled to the allowances a foster carer or even a kinship carer might receive. Some parents were very angry that children who were so difficult that they could not be placed in a foster family were returned to them with little support, particularly little financial support.

> You know I have told her (social worker), 'You come and dump one of my kids here, totally out of the blue, leave us here scrimping and bloody scraping'. Literally I nearly had to go out and thieve again it got that bad.

However, it was possible to see very contrasting outcomes of these returns home. One boy appeared to have settled at home much better than had been expected and got a job. But for other parents it was hard having a difficult teenager back when they had perhaps managed to establish a stable life only in the absence of parenting responsibilities.

> We have been on our own all those years and suddenly having a kid back…well I like it but when he has his friends in, that gets Derek down. (Tina)

It was difficult after this gap while children were away to establish their authority as parents or perhaps to put their own guilt aside in order to set limits or assert their own needs. It must also be difficult for children to know how to handle this new situation.

The impact of bringing up subsequent children

There were several parents who had met new, stable partners and had gone on to have children whom they cared for successfully. This in turn impacted on their feelings about the children whom they had not been able to care for and who were in foster care.

In one case, a mother had chosen to withdraw from care proceedings for her older children, in recognition of the fact that she stood some chance of keeping the younger child or future children, but this may have been at risk if she had to care for the older, already difficult children as well. Kathy was asked whether caring for her two small boys at home had affected her feelings about her older children.

> Of course it does, no one is ever, ever, ever going to get over that guilt. These boys have everything and will continue to. I just wish it could have been like that for the others. It can't be now. I can only try to put right what I have done and in trying to put that right, make sure that these two never suffer. And I can do my best for Olivia and Anna now, you know, and that is all I can do.

There were a number of cases where members of sibling groups were in very different situations, where younger siblings of fostered children lived at home or had been adopted, where older siblings had never been in care or where other siblings of any age had gone to live with relatives. This affected how parents experienced the placements of those children in foster care and their parenting role for those at home. Although parents may grieve for the loss of the child or children in care, the opportunity to become a successful parent to subsequent children gave some parents a very different sense of themselves than was possible for those for whom their only chance to be a proper parent had been lost.

How parents think their children feel about them

It was not easy for parents to be sure how their children felt about them – and few were able to comment. But Kathy did reflect on this difficult issue and her children's mixed feelings.

> I just think they hate me, but I also know deep down because… Keith has said to the social worker, 'How is my mum? I know all the things that she has done and what has happened, but she is still my mum.'

But some children are still said to be angry.

> He took on a lot of responsibility when I ended up going to jail, being the oldest boy I suppose or the eldest kid he sort of, I suppose tried to take my place, so he took a hell of a lot on board I think and I think yes. I think he is quite an angry boy actually, he has got a lot of things he needs to deal with by himself. (Jack)

When the children are upset or angry, the past may be thrown back at the parents.

> In every argument it will always be 'Well you were a junkie' and I will have that to my dying day… I think that is their ultimate weapon you know, yeah. (Tina)

The question of who was to blame for the children being in care is difficult for children as well as parents, but the views of both can change over time.

> But none of them blame me for it now. You know, they say 'We don't blame you for putting us in care mum, that weren't your fault. Obviously you weren't well'. And they will be able to read my files when they get older and their own, you know. (Lorraine)

Parents and children need to agree a story that helps them to manage their shared family history and the reason for the separation. But in particular what helped parents was the feeling that they had the understanding and forgiveness of their children. This could sometimes best be achieved through negotiation, in which parents accepted some responsibility, thus giving the children a more coherent narrative that fitted their memory. Kathy described how she felt when her 18-year-old daughter, Anna, asked to see her, having not wanted contact for two years.

> Over the moon, over the moon. We are now building that relationship. We have talked at some length… She said, 'I don't blame you mum, you were ill', but I turned round and said, 'I might have been ill, Anna, but it was my job to look after you'. So we sort of met each other half way. She has forgiven me and

she sees things completely differently this time. We are gradually rebuilding it, bit by bit. Nothing is going to happen overnight, but we will get there. She can say, 'I love you mum'. I am honoured because I have been given a second chance. (Kathy)

Conclusion

Parents' experiences and perceptions of their children growing up in foster care varied and evolved over time. It is perhaps possible to think of some of these changes in terms of parents coming to terms with their loss and moving on. But although feelings of grief and anger may have softened and parents may not be as preoccupied with the loss, for most parents the knowledge that their children are out there, living in a different family, leading lives about which they generally could know only a limited amount, is a source of sadness and regret. But the quality of parents' current lives, their involvement with new partners or in caring for subsequent children could make a difference – as could the quality of their contact and their relationships with foster carers and social workers, which the following chapters will explore.

Parents' perspectives on their children growing up in foster care: key themes and implications for practice

- The loss of a child into care is like a bereavement. But like a bereavement, parents' experience of this loss is felt and expressed in different ways, which often evolve over the years that their children are in care. Social workers need to recognise and acknowledge the complex and often contradictory feelings that each parent experiences in the face of a loss that is accompanied by feelings of powerlessness and stigma.

- The nature and intensity of the experience of loss is affected by a range of emotional and cognitive appraisal factors that characterise parents' reactions to children being in care; these might be feelings of regret and self-blame, for example, or anger at a partner or professional, or a combination. Social workers may therefore be dealing with parents who have a profound sense of grief and low self-esteem. These feelings need to be expressed. But parents can also be encouraged to take what is positive from the situation, in terms perhaps of recognising the moments when children were happy in their care, and when they had done their best for them. It may also be possible to help parents resolve their feelings of loss by being able to take pride in the progress they have made while in care.

• Where parents perceive children as settled and thriving in foster care, they are often able to find ways to accept the situation, whether or not they feel that the original move into care was necessary. But for some parents, even where children do well in care, there is ongoing anger and resentment.

• Where children have not thrived in care and perhaps have multiple placements, parents feel an understandable combination of anger and concern. Some see these failures of the system to achieve a settled placement as further evidence that the children should not be in care and do not want to be in care. Social workers will be experiencing their own feelings of concern and frustration when it has proved difficult to find the right placement for a child or when placements end unhappily. Where parents are also critical of what is happening for children, it can make it additionally challenging for social workers to defend the original decision for children to be in care.

• The role that parents are expected to play when children are in long-term care will need to be defined by the care plan and the placement plan, as parents are often not sure what role they will, can or should have.

• Supervision to help practitioners remain thoughtful, balanced and empathic is particularly necessary in managing the relationship with parents in the longer term, while retaining a focus on the welfare of the child.

5

Contact Between Parents and Their Children

Contact between parents and their children in foster care is the thread that in most cases keeps their relationship alive. Seeing the children, speaking to them on the phone, writing them letters or giving them Christmas and birthday presents, these are the experiences that help mothers and fathers to feel connected to their sons and daughters and are key to the extent to which they can feel and act as parents. On the other hand, each contact visit or phone call or letter is additionally a reminder that their relationship with the child and their role as parent is from a distance and not like that of other parents. Although contact with children may be promoted and facilitated by the local authority, it is also regulated and controlled in most respects. Although for some parents contact with their children was an easy and relaxed experience, for most it was something that, however valued, had to be carefully negotiated and managed, practically and, above all, emotionally, through the days, weeks, months and years that their children were in foster care.

Contact for children in care has proved one of the most complex areas to understand and about which practice decisions have to be made (Cleaver 2000; Schofield and Stevenson 2009; Sinclair 2005). The child's 'needs' and 'rights' to have contact are set out in the Children Act 1989 and associated guidance, which built on research (e.g. Rowe, Hundley and Garnett 1989; Thoburn 1991) that highlighted the importance of the birth family in the lives of children in care. For children who are in long-term care, the importance of contact has to be seen in the context of other policy and practice imperatives – in particular, the local authority's duty as corporate parent to promote the welfare of the child and to agree and support a *permanency* plan.

But these legal, policy, research and practice contexts do not provide an answer to the most simple and yet challenging of questions about contact for each child – with whom, how often, where, and with or without supervision? Rules of thumb are no help; professional judgements in each case have to be made (Sinclair 2005). Judgements about what children need in relation to contact with their parents (and siblings, grandparents and other relatives) have to take into account the balance in long-term placements between promoting the security and well-being of the child while minimising any risk of harm to the child or the placement (Beek and Schofield 2004b; Schofield and Stevenson 2009). Key factors in the child, the birth family, the foster family and the local authority that make up this balance will also change over the life of a placement and so need constant review.

Such practice questions for social workers have implications for how parents experience contact. Contact decisions and some of the reasons for contact arrangements had generally been explained to parents. Where contact was relaxed and parents had easy relationships with foster carers, the arrangements and the reasons for them were easy to understand, accept and live with. Parents in these cases were often grateful for the support for contact they received from social workers and carers. But, as we shall see, there are many situations when parents live within a regulated programme of contact that they found hard to understand in common-sense terms, or to live with in terms of their sense of themselves as parents. It is often not easy for parents to make sense of a plan for contact with their children that is restricted to every three months or is supervised in a family centre, both of which suggest that their children need only a limited amount of time with them or need to be protected from what they might say or do. From the backgrounds of these children, even as described by the parents themselves, it is not hard to see why some restrictions might apply in the context of a plan for the child to become a member of the foster family. On the other hand where there were restrictions, for the parent in question, these could seem hard to accept.

Whatever the context, contact can be a difficult emotional mix of a range of feelings; for example, anxiety in anticipation, relief when the children seem pleased to see you, pleasure at how lovely the children look, humiliation that you cannot be trusted unsupervised, and sadness when it is time to say good-bye.

Contact in the early days of placement – and how it might change

When children are away from their parents and in foster care, those first experiences of contact can be particularly hard for parents to manage.

> It didn't feel the same at all. It was upsetting because Megan used to wave to me 'Bye Mummy', and I would have to leave them. And then I would go home and have all photos around me and then I would think of them, how they were at night going to bed, you know, just mother's instincts and everything.

Annette could recognise that the children had been at risk or actually harmed as a result of problems while in her care. But for her to see her children briefly and then for the children to wave good-bye to her, with their foster carer not their mother putting them to bed at night, was nonetheless a distressing change.

For Amy who had been imprisoned (for an offence unrelated to her parenting) there was a gap of two months before she could see her daughter and she was afraid that Jessica would not recognise her.

> It was terrible, I can't explain it. It was just inside my head. I am just thinking, she is not going to know me, she is not going to recognise me, she is just going to forget me… And then eventually when she did come I was stood at the gate and she saw me and she just shouted my name at the top of her voice and she just grabbed hold of me and she wouldn't let go, you know, and she was only, she had just turned two, and then she just burst out crying.

During this early period of children being in care, contact for most parents was quite frequent, because assessment and then court proceedings meant that there was still a possibility, until a final order was made, that children might return home. Positive accounts were sometimes given by parents of the relaxed and inclusive approach of the foster carers at this stage (see later chapter on foster carers), with placements often quite close geographically to the parents in order to facilitate contact. But once there was a plan for long-term foster care, whether made at court or subsequently, contact was likely to reduce, and it was not unusual for children's permanent placements to be at some distance from the birth family.

Paula accepted the need for her daughter Alice to be in care, as she had not bonded with her and felt she could neither love her fully nor manage her behaviour. So, she says, 'we' made the decision for long-term foster care, and she accepts the implications for more limited contact.

> Yes contact is now less than it was. It was sort of like once a week at first, and then it sort of started tailing off, once we had made the decision for her to stay in foster care… Now it has got to the point where it is once a month for all of us and now it looks like it is going to be once every sort of two possibly even three months between contact. But there is a big difference where she is living now, which is a long way. And the amount of time she is actually going to get to see us is probably going to be shorter than the amount of time the whole round trip is going to take us.

This weighing up of the evolving contact situation is by a mother who has struggled to come to terms with the many losses in her life, including the cot death of her first child. But the tone is not untypical of other parents who, in some senses, have had (at some level) to let children go. Paula was in a situation where Alice was growing up in foster care, but her other young children were at home. Her task was therefore to make the most of contact when it happened and to accept that the drift of the older child away from them, emotionally and in terms of her identity in the new family, was inevitable.

The initial reduction in contact frequency that sometimes happened when placements became long-term or permanent would, however, not necessarily persist once children were older, were to have their own telephone contact, were seen to be less at risk of harm through contact or were no longer seen as in need of supervision. So change over time was not only in the direction of less contact, with reductions at an earlier stage sometimes reversed in the teenage years.

> Well I can ring Brendan now when I like and that. When I was first seeing him it was with my social worker at first. But because Brendan is getting a bit older he wanted to see me and Eric on our own without the social worker there. So Cynthia (foster carer) meets me, leaves me and Eric to see him and that so we can spend time.

In adolescence, as at other ages, there is variation in the pattern of contact, which appeared to depend mainly on the quality of the child's relationships in the foster and birth families and resources available, but sometimes seemed to be for historic reasons. Some children developed closer relationships with their parents in adolescence, which affected and was affected by frequency of contact. But there were also children who grew closer to the foster parents over time and, because they identified more with the foster family in adolescence, chose to have less or no contact with parents. Some parents accepted this and moved on, while others grieved for another loss.

The role of older children in making choices about contact emerged in different ways. There were a number of cases where parents reported that teenage children were choosing whether to have contact, and how frequently that would be. In some cases, parents expressed the idea that it was better for children to choose freely whether to see them, as this father describes:

> It's very up and down at the moment, especially our two oldest boys, Gavin and Evan. Now I haven't spoken to Gavin for twelve months, a year… It was before Christmas, four or five months since I last spoke to Evan. We went and had a visit with him and that went perfectly well, we had a good day and haven't heard from him since. I don't push myself on the kids, I don't hassle them, get on the phone and hassle them or anything like that. I just let them come to me when they are ready, because I feel at the end of the day if they don't want to speak to me then there is a reason for that, do you know what I mean? I don't sort of get in their face and want to know why. I mean they have got enough problems and even things to think about, not being at home. If they are not contacting me then there is a reason for it and I would rather them get over that reason and come to me when they are ready. So we just haven't had no contact at all for a while. (Eddie)

In some senses these older children were being allowed to 'choose' whether to have contact, but equally, the parents were expecting the children to make the first move and so leaving the responsibility with them. The fact that parents were not asking to see their children might be interpreted as empowering them or perhaps giving them the freedom to settle in their foster family. But the lack of initiative by the parents in seeking contact may well be interpreted differently by the children, the foster carers and the social workers – perhaps as lack of interest or commitment. These decisions about who should make the first move, the parent or the child, are always difficult in contact situations – the same dilemmas regularly surface in contact after divorce. But the interpretation of activity or non-activity by parents or children is not always predictable and for social workers it is rarely easy to know how to approach these situations and whether to intervene to set up contact or to accept the way in which the child–parent relationship appears to be evolving.

For some parents, the fact that their children actively expressed a wish not to see them was very painful. Gina tried to communicate by letter in order to bridge the gap.

> I still want her to know I love her, because I don't know what she is being told you see, so I still want her to know I love her, but I don't know if the letters are even getting to her or not.

Philip and Caroline had struggled as parents with a combination of drug addiction and the sudden death of his wife's mother. When their children went into care, Philip was devastated. He has remained in a traumatised state. Hs marriage ended, he spent time in prison and has had a continuous struggle with both drugs and depression. The hope that one day he can get his children back was the focus of his life and, he said, gave him something to live for. At the time of the interview, two of his three children were refusing to see him. As well as making him sad and angry, and concerned that his children may be influenced negatively towards him by carers or social workers, this also had the effect of making his contact with the remaining child, his 'princess', even more significant. But of course, such investment in this one child may place expectations on her that she cannot fulfil and which she may find difficult to manage as she gets older.

This was one of many accounts of the significance of contact with individual children in the lives of parents, where, although we were only hearing the parent's perspective, it was apparent that these hopes and preoccupations must be having some impact on the child. Both parent and child would need support from social workers (and foster carers) to manage the weight of expectations.

Contact arrangements: where do we go and what do we do?

Before looking at the arrangements for contact, it is worth thinking about the question of who decides on the venue and the activities. For some parents, there was a choice.

> The social worker says, 'Where do you like to go?' I say, 'Ask the girls'. I will do anything that the girls want to do. (Lorraine)

Parents involved in making these choices, however, said that it was not always easy or straightforward to choose contact activities, as these needed to be planned and booked. Lorraine commented that it was nice to be outside with the children, but could this be planned ahead?

> Then you have got to have the weather, you have got to know what the weather is going to be like, because contacts have to be planned in advance, they have got to pre-book them. So if you don't know what the weather is going to be we like to do things inside so the kids are going to be dry.

As with other aspects of their parenting, it was not often possible to act spontaneously in relation to contact and it could be difficult for arrangements to be flexible, especially where supervision was required, even if parents, the children and the social workers might have preferred this.

The parents' accounts of face-to-face contact, their meetings with their children, did suggest a range of venues and activities, all of which provided different kinds of experience. Where the children were older and the relationships all round were relaxed, parents and children could take advantage of a range of opportunities to meet. In this account, they could meet up at the foster family's beach chalet and for weekend staying contact.

> We go on the beach and when they are staying at the chalet we will go down there. We visit Ian and we will go into the local town and then drop him off and come home. With Robert we either go to the cinema or come back here and he will stay the weekend and usually play PlayStation or something with his brother. (Gemma)

Parents commented on the preparations they might make to help everyone get the most from contact. These examples again are of older children and relaxed, unsupervised contact, which allowed parents to do 'ordinary' things with their teenage children, which Gina valued.

> We take board games and Gerald (partner) takes his PSP and Rhys likes to send messages on my phone and play games that I have got on my phone. And you know we take board games and we take the dog for a walk or we'll go into town sometimes and go shopping, take him shopping and stuff, which he absolutely loves to do.

Very ordinary things can have significance for family relationships and family membership, and for some parents providing food for their children was an important part of making contact a family occasion. For one family, food was part of a varied programme that could be planned for, with the father making his contribution.

> Derek never cooks at home but he ended up cooking all the pancakes at the family centre. She (social worker) has planned contact throughout the year right up to Christmas and we have got a few at the bowling alley, we have got the Valley Park and then the Christmas visit is at the family centre... At the Christmas visit we do like a little bit of food, like a little buffet and we take our presents for the kids. It is normally like two days before Christmas, but we let them open their presents there and then. (Tina)

Tina and her husband, both with difficult histories of drug addiction but who are now drug free, attempt to give and to get the very best they can out of their contact visits. Unusually in the sample, they are both the biological parents of the children in care and they have stayed together. They support each other in managing and accepting their loss, but also in enjoying what relationship they can sustain as parents through contact and through helping their children enjoy being with them. But this programme of contact relies on the active involvement of the social worker.

For parents what was probably most important was to feel that they could make choices about contact that would create the feel of a 'real' family outing.

> The social worker said during the six weeks holiday we can meet up at the woods, to take the dog for a walk. So it's part of our family thing, do you know what I mean? So we can suggest things and the social worker is quite good, she will say yes you can take

the dog for a walk down to the woods or what have you and we'll meet you there and you can have a picnic, which is quite good. (Gina)

This case-responsible social worker was well known to the parents and was often directly involved with contact, a situation that is not so common now when contact centres and family support workers are more likely to support and supervise contact.

Contact might also be very flexible, with little involvement from social work services, where there was a contact parent who had not been the focus of concerns, as this father, Darren, reported.

Daisy was living down the road from here and I was having access whenever I wanted basically. If I wanted to go down and see her it was not a problem, I just phoned up Bernice (carer) who was looking after her or went down and saw her, no problem at all.

For these informal unsupervised arrangements to work, both carers and social workers needed to be flexible and to trust the parents, and parents needed to demonstrate their trustworthiness. But flexibility was most likely when parents had direct relationships with foster carers and contact was organised between them.

Although some contact was more flexible when parents and carers had a relationship, contact that included visiting the foster home was rare. Louise described how much she valued it, although acknowledging that her daughter, Ella, also liked time alone away from the foster home.

When I turn up at the house, you know I am very invited, I am very welcome. I think you know Ella likes to get out. She will bring me up to her room and she will show me her work and we will probably go for a walk along the beach and stuff like that. Anthea (foster carer) is really accommodating. She doesn't really expect us back. She just lets us…so you know the contact is very positive.

Given the range of agencies and people involved in a placement, not all contact arrangements were simple to negotiate, neither in the early days nor as children got older and their needs and circumstances changed. Parents described having to be active to get the arrangements they liked or felt suited the children. Louise had to negotiate with a number of agencies and individuals.

There were lots of different agencies, it wasn't just as simple as one social worker, it might be link workers, carers. So you know there were times when I had to, not complain, but I had to write letters and say can't we do this a little bit better? I just wanted to see my child and I am willing to go to any lengths really.

The cost of contact

For some parents, the more enjoyable activities at contact could create other problems – the cost. This was particularly frustrating when parents had previously had funding that had been cut. Gemma was disappointed and angry.

Previously whenever we had contact social services would help us with the cost of days out like transport and all that. We all went to the country park and social services paid for it and it was a lovely day out. … The next contact we were due to have was going to be at the zoo, but they said we can't afford it because they have cut back our expenses, so we are not allowed to do it no more. If your kids are in foster care now you have to provide all the contact fees. No parent with kids in foster care can afford it.

These expensive days out multiplied across a local authority would clearly be putting pressure on budgets, but from the parents' and children's point of view they made a potentially awkward situation rewarding and memorable. From the local authority's point of view they were also likely to be supporting trips out or holidays for the children with the foster family too. Budget holders may have to see the whole situation when they allocate resources, but for parents with limited contact it was hard to see it that way.

The cost of contact had implications for other aspects of the arrangements, in particular, as Lorraine pointed out, the importance of having a contact programme in advance so that parents could save up.

I get a letter a week in advance. But they always promise me that I will have certain times written down so that I can put it up on my notice board, so that I know in advance, so it is not just a one off letter. Because I like to have money, for when I go out. If I have got the money, I like to buy them an ice-cream or Jed (partner) will put 50p in a teddy machine and win them teddies. So they always go back with something from me and Jed.

Travel and preparation for contact

Decisions about where contact would happen often had to include considerations about whether children should travel to where parents are, parents should travel to near children's foster homes or parents and children could meet in the middle. Some parents asked for contact to be where it would be best for the children. Lorraine wanted contact to be as good as possible.

> I said you know it is not fair for the girls to come all the way down here after school or even if it is a school holiday, travel all the way here to do nothing because there is nothing here for them. So I said, I will do all the travelling for them, we will go to the town near them. There is more to do there and because the kids live near they are not going to be tired through the travelling, you know, we can have a brilliant contact.

The decisions about travel arrangements might be a comfortable negotiation, with parents feeling consulted and involved. But for some parents, the process of getting to contact was emotionally challenging, with difficult travel arrangements adding to the stress. The quality of contact, in particular how the parent might seem to the children, could be affected by the arrangements. Tina, whose mental health difficulties included agoraphobia, reflected on both the emotional pressure and level of anxiety, and how much better it was for her when she could get to contact with less difficulty.

> It was a lot worse when I had that long train journey. When they started the visits near me just recently, the social worker said, I have never seen you look so refreshed. I said that is because I haven't had to sit on a train for two hours to get here. When I used to go to the other place, I used to get up at half three in the morning just to get built up to leave here at quarter past eight… I could never like be in bed and my husband saying well we have got to go in an hour, I just wouldn't get there. I have to build myself up every time I leave the house.

Physical health problems were also common among parents and sometimes caused problems with travel to contact. Eddie was angry about the fact that, in spite of his health, he was expected to travel some distance for contact, which was near to where the children were living.

I have got ill health and I am on long term sick. I get quite bad with my chest and sometimes I can't travel distances and they were making me go to the city, you know, and I was finding it absolutely horrendous because I was having to leave here early in the morning, do like two hours on the train going over, have the visit with the kids and then have a two hour train coming back and then I had to walk from the train station home and I was physically coming home absolutely worn out and sick for days.

This father complained until the arrangements were changed. As discussed in the later chapter on the relationships with social workers, it was difficult for parents to know how pushy to be about contact arrangements – if they demanded or got angry it might produce results, but it might lead to some lack of trust by social workers about what might happen at contact, and parents were concerned it could lead to more restrictions. But for social workers, too, it would obviously not always be easy to know how to do what was best for children and for parents. The need to avoid lengthy journeys for children might clash with parents' wishes and needs. The life of the foster family would also have to be taken into account by social workers, as foster families may have regular activities at a weekend or at half term that a whole day at contact for perhaps one of several children may disrupt. Any threat to the placement that contact arrangements might represent would, therefore, also have to be taken into account.

Contact is an area where the difficulty of making the right decisions, even about the most basic arrangements, is profoundly affected by many factors in the children, the carers and the parents themselves. Even decisions about choice of placement have to take to account travel time for contact, although this should be weighed against the prospect of a well-matched long-term placement for the child, where contact may be only four to six times a year.

The role of supervision of contact

Supervision of contact was a very important issue for parents, although it was seen by some as necessary and helpful, by some as acceptable but constraining, and by others as an unnecessary evil.

Often a pattern of supervised contact had developed during the early stages of placement when children were first removed and were going through court and assessments. Whether contact continued to be supervised over the years did seem to vary, in most cases depending on factors such as the age of the child, the characteristics of the contact parent and the relationship between parents and carers – although it seemed likely from the various accounts that judgements about the need for supervision, and reviews of those judgements, varied between and within local authorities. One difficulty is that once supervision is removed, it can become difficult to reinstate, so decisions tend to be cautious.

In the examples in the previous section of varied trips and pancake making, contact was actually 'supervised' in most cases. But in those cases supervision also meant facilitation, in that the focus appeared to be at least as much on helping the parents to enjoy and manage the children. Supervision to help manage behaviour could apply even with one child, where it might be perceived by parents as a form of support with a difficult child or one difficult child in a sibling group.

> The social worker stayed with us because we still had, even the foster carers had, problems with Ian at the time. (Gemma)

For some parents, supervision, or at least the presence of a social worker, was beneficial because they did not feel confident or competent in keeping the children occupied.

> I mean I can accept supervised visits. To be honest with you, I wouldn't want a visit where I just had the kids on my own, because I wouldn't have a clue what to do. (Tina)

It is not surprising that parents who are separated from their children find it hard to keep in touch with activities that the child likes or are age appropriate, or find it hard to manage siblings with different needs coming from different placements.

Other parents felt that supervision could be tolerated as long as it was unobtrusive.

> We have got an hour and a half, and even if they are in the background the social workers can be there, but you know so they are not right beside us listening to everything you know. (Lorraine)

In one case a parent felt it was beneficial for the social worker supervising contact to be unobtrusive, but also to be part of the family gathering some of the time.

> She doesn't like hover right next to us do you know what I mean, she will like hover in the background. But we keep her involved because we like Rhys to know that we get on, you know. (Gina)

Where supervision was obtrusive, children were also said to find supervision difficult.

> Julian stated that he don't want the social worker. We did have a social worker come down for three weeks following us around, watching our every move and doing this and doing that and doing the other, she drove us mad. (Helen)

But supervision at a family centre venue could be so difficult when children were also restless that parents said they would not want contact more than every three months.

> It is all frustration when it is in a little room, because when I see the kids I am happy for twenty minutes and then I am getting bored because I am in this room and they are getting bored as well. They play with toys and then they want to move on to something else and they can't move on from what is in the room. They get frustrated, run up and down, make a mess of the place you know. It is not easy. (Winston)

But other supervised contact venues that were for activities could also feel unsatisfactory if used repeatedly, with the supervision and lack of trust being an extra objection.

> Bowling! Every flaming time I have a visit they get me at a flaming bowling centre. You know you would think really at the end of the day, I see them three times a year, you would think they would vary it a bit, take them down the flaming beach or something or whatever. It is always at a bowling centre for some reason. I don't know whether it is because it is an enclosed area or something because they think I am going to run off with the kids. I don't know but it is always bowling! (Eddie)

Bowling alleys featured quite frequently as a venue for contact for a number of families in different local authorities, often where older sibling groups needed to meet together. The dilemma is always how to find venues that meet the needs of children of different ages, allow for some kind of supervision or support, but also ensure that parents can give children the best experience that is possible, under the circumstances.

However much supervision could be used quite flexibly and sensitively by social workers, parents who had moved from supervised to unsupervised contact reflected on how much they had previously been affected by the restrictions of supervision.

> It is lovely now, it is very relaxed... Basically I feel like a mum again and I don't with the Local Authority there, I don't feel like a mum. (Alison)

Rules for contact

Often linked to supervised contact, although sometimes applying also to unsupervised contact, were unwritten 'rules' about what could be discussed by parents and children at contact. There is often so much emotion for the children that is bubbling under the surface, but when it is expressed at contact there is not always time to resolve it and then there may be a long time till they are together again. But the rules dictated what could be talked about at contact and limited the opportunities for the parent to get to grips with and maybe help resolve what is distressing the child.

> I would admit, out of all my children, one minute I could go on contact with Bryony and she would be as right as rain, and then the next minute it is like she is hurt, she is upset, she don't understand. And of course we are not allowed to discuss things in depth, and because we only get two hours it is not enough to talk about that anyway. So, yes, once every three months is not a long time to talk and that is why I feel about the bond going. (Jenny)

The restriction on discussing difficult questions about the past – such as what happened prior to the child coming into care, why the child is in care and so on – is likely to be based on concerns that this will upset the child, that the parent may present themselves in a positive light that is not accurate or perhaps talk negatively about social workers or foster carers. But these restrictions created some real difficulties.

> Dena (social worker) trusts me but as I say they have rules that you are not allowed to talk about their dad and things like that. I find it really strange because there are sort of all rules for all of us really.

And what would you like to talk to them about that you can't at the moment?

Well things like what they are doing with their lives and what they want to do and how they feel about actually being in care, because it is not a nice thing to talk about, but I think it would help them if they could talk to me about it but they can't. Like when I asked them where they were going abroad, they are not allowed to tell me where they are going, they looked at Dena first. But they are going to Spain, they said in the end, but they had to have permission even to say that. I think there have been so many things happen to children in care they just think you are going to take them which is understandable because lots of people have tried to do that so much, I do understand all that. But I just think you know they should be more, I don't know trust you a bit, you know give you a bit more leeway and everything. (Annette)

Here the rules about what could be talked about and a general level of secrecy applied not just to past events but to current and future events. For some parents, these restrictions meant that it was almost impossible to be a proper parent, because you were not allowed to know about what the children were really thinking or feeling.

Now to me that is stupid because how are you meant to get the understanding of what your kids are going through when there are so many things I am not meant to talk to them about and that? It is madness; it really is crazy when you think about it, because I need to get a better understanding. Of course I want to know why they don't phone me, why they don't write. I write to them, but even my writing has got a bit less now, because yeah I get upset and all that and I get hurt that they don't write back and that and obviously I feel that they must have a reason but I can't ask them for that reason. (Jenny)

Some restrictions may be understandable and appropriate, in some situations and at some stages. On the other hand, carefully managed and facilitated contact meetings at which these important questions about the past and the present can be discussed, with both child and parent prepared before the meeting, would almost certainly help both parent and child to say some necessary and important things to each other that would perhaps help both to move on emotionally and in their lives. This kind of meeting would not, of course, be at every contact, but might be needed at intervals during a child's childhood in foster care. As the child gets older and more settled, he or she may become developmentally better able to ask these questions and to understand possible answers with increasing degrees of sophistication, but also to feel empathy for the parent – and parents may also become better able to reflect on the past and be more open and able to help the child.

All the work that may be done by social workers with children and sometimes, though less often, with parents to resolve ideas and feelings from the past, might be helped if it were possible to bring parents and children together with therapeutic goals in mind. Parents see children either at LAC reviews (when it is not appropriate to do this kind of work and in fact parents may feel drawn into a more antagonistic or demanding stance *vis-à-vis* the professionals) or at a bowling alley or contact activity (where again useful talking about difficult matters is less likely).

Sibling groups

One of the most powerful features of accounts given by parents was the impact of complex sibling groups on their efforts to manage their role as parents and their relationships with their individual children, and this was particularly evident at contact.

In all families, parents' feelings about each of their children may vary. Responding to children's different personalities and meeting their different needs, being fair to each child, is a challenge for any parent. Siblings' feelings about each other, for example, and about which child is seen as favoured or rejected by parents, also run deep and can last into adulthood.

However, these 'normal' family tensions are played out in very complicated ways for parents and children when, for example, there are six children in a sibling group of whom the eldest lives with an ex-partner, the next eldest child has left care and is at home, the two next children are in long-term foster care and the youngest is about to be adopted. What is more, in most, but not all, of these larger families, children were from different fathers, which added additional emotional and loyalty dynamics to the mix. Even where children were from the same father, some children were apparently favoured, which left already anxious, separated children feeling distressed and angry.

> Their dad is still close to Malcolm. He sees him once every fortnight on a Saturday. He has got a bond with Malcolm, because he is sixteen and he can have a chat with him, take him out and places and he go and whatever. But for the other three he hasn't bought Christmas presents, birthday presents and that is why Jake is so angry now, because he thinks that his dad hates him. (Lorraine)

Although for some sibling groups all children were in long-term foster families, combinations of different placement types were not unusual. And even where children were in the same placement type, contact arrangements and relationship quality could, of course, vary. Tina and Derek had diverse contact arrangements with their children that did not make too much sense to them, and then an older child was returned to them. Although the needs of their children of different ages and in different placements were different, from their point of view the arrangements were hard to accept.

> I have to see two of my kids under supervised access and the other two, one lives here and one comes here daily, so it just seems crazy really.

Although the goal of having the siblings together for contact with parents was often shared by social workers and parents (as it allowed the family to be a family, gave siblings contact with each other and was efficient for everyone in terms of time) it was often seen by parents as not necessarily meeting their needs or the needs of individual children. Sometimes, this was because the time was just not enough, as this father describes.

> I was seeing them altogether, all six of them at once. But I have now asked for that to be separated, because I was finding it really difficult because basically they only give me an hour and half on the visits. (Eddie)

What would be a short visit for a father to fit in conversation and a relationship with a number of children may be as long as the children themselves could manage, so social workers had to prioritise what was possible. But parents often asked for and had separate contact visits with each child, or separate time within visits, so that they could be sure that each child had their needs met.

> Yesterday I got to see Jake, took him out to McDonalds on my own for an hour and a half. I want to do that with the girls so they (children's services) can trust me to see that I can look after them. But because Kirsty wants mummy time and so does Sabrina, me and Jed (partner) share it while the social workers are with us. So Kirsty has got mummy time and she can speak to me about anything that is going on while Sabrina is playing bowling with Jed, and then vice versa, we swap… (Lorraine)

Some of the concerns about seeing siblings together and the possible need for separate contact is about the possibility of sibling disputes arising. This adds to the more obvious anxieties at contact about how the children will be and how they will react to seeing the parents.

> But I always think something is going to go wrong, because we have had two really upsetting visits when Elliot (older son not in care) has been there, where they all kicked off. How we never got banned from that place I will never know. (Tina)

In some cases, contact plans may be affected by the behaviour of an older sibling at home who might also 'kick off'.

> I mean I am not even allowed to have Isabel and Joe come over for visits at the moment while Brett is here in case he kicks off. He doesn't drink a lot but when he has too much to drink he will kick off. (Karen)

One of the differences that also had to be managed by parents was the different reactions that siblings had to them.

> It is hard, really, really hard. Lewis kisses and cuddles me and says, 'Alright mum see you later'. But Fraser clings on to me and keeps running back and cuddling me, and saying, 'I love you mum, thank you for this', and it is ever so hard to let go. (Helen)

In this case it is the older brother, Fraser, who shows his feelings most at separation, and the mother believed it was perhaps because the younger brother, Lewis, had been removed when he was only a baby. But this difference in the children's reactions also means that she may feel rather less connected to the younger child as a mother, a difference that could persist as children show differing degrees of 'loyalty' to the birth and the foster parents.

One of the most difficult sibling factors to manage is that strong feelings are aroused for the children in foster care when they have a brother or sister living with the birth parents. This may affect not only the contact visits themselves, but also the child's relationships in the foster family. This can occur when there are older siblings who were perhaps never in care and live with a father or grandparent, children who were born of a subsequent relationship and were never taken into care, or older siblings who have returned home. Children's behaviour may be difficult at contact or just after, as in this case where two children are in foster care, but their sibling was never in care and lives with their father. Steve describes his fostered daughter's reaction after contact.

> Whitney goes into the foster home sobbing sometimes after contact saying, 'I want my dad, I want my dad, I want my dad'.

There may be problems in the placement after contact when one child has returned from care to the parent.

> Every time I go on a family visit and we are all there together, like the six kids and me, then Kieran walks away with me and comes home with me at night and the others don't see us again for another three or four month. Of course that is doing their heads in proper, you know. I think that is why Katrina is kicking off so much at the moment because she wants to come home. (Eddie)

For some children, contact was a time to express anger towards the parent.

> Keith was going through a stage and went to me, 'You lied to me'. I said 'Why did I lie to you, what did I say?' He went, 'Well you said Social Services took me into care, but they didn't. You put me into care!' I went 'No'…and it is things like that. I think he was resenting me because he was in foster care maybe. (Sophie)

Sometimes all the children would be showing different emotions when they met at contact. Supervision (by a foster carer) was available, but the situation still got out of hand and Sophie was physically and emotionally hurt.

> There was one day that I wanted to end the contact there and then, because I was upset, Kayleigh was upset, Erin was upset, my niece was upset. Len was calming Keith down…and Cheryl

> (carer) she was just walking about like saying, 'What's going on?'
> I tried to calm Keith down, but I got punched in the face a couple
> of times so I thought…it was just really upsetting.

After contact like this parents and children need time to recover, opportunities to resolve their feelings and strategies to repair the relationships. The presence of the carer might mean that she would be able to talk through the difficult visit with the children in her care, though siblings from different placements might have less support unless this carer communicated with the other carers. But for the parents, unless the social worker heard about the contact and/or checked to see how they were feeling, there might not be opportunities to pick up the pieces and work towards the next contact.

Telephone contact

Most of the discussion so far has focussed on face-to-face contact. But for many parents, telephone contact played as important if not more important a role in developing and maintaining a relationship with their children. The situation in relation to contact has been radically altered by the presence of mobile phones in the lives of older children and young people. Providing as it does a good way for carers to keep in touch with children, the mobile phone inevitably also means that children can be reached by and can reach their parents at times and frequencies that are far beyond the level of contact plans and agreements.

For most parents, where telephone contact featured in the contact plan, it would usually be one of a range of forms of contact.

> I speak to them every four weeks on the phone and I go and have
> contact. We write letters regularly and I buy them presents. I send
> them money for their birthday and Christmas. (Lorraine)

For parents and older children, in particular where placements are at a distance or they had other commitments, the phone was a good way to keep in very regular contact – as it would be in all families.

> He phones me once a week. I saw him when he was up for the
> last half term at the end of May. He come for the whole half term
> because he started his job on the 7th June and because he has
> to work six days a week he said he won't be able to get up here
> until August, September time when it finishes. So I said to him just

> make sure you phone me once a week so I know you are alright
> so he does that. (Karen)

But for some parents, the mobile phone led to frequent contacts. One mother phoned her teenage son every day, when he got in from school and at bedtime, a level of contact that she (and at least one other mother) defined as right for a mother to have. But this constant contact at sensitive times of day perpetuated her sense that she was the most important person in his life, as he appeared to be in hers, but must have left him with a significant emotional burden of expectation.

As with other aspects of contact, telephone contact was more regulated in some placements than others and worked out differently with different siblings. In some cases, telephone calls were seen as an easy, untroubling communication with one sibling, but a high risk activity with other siblings who showed distress afterwards. Lorraine had to accept different arrangements.

> I can phone Jake every week but the girls every four weeks, because that takes them four weeks to get over the phone call. They described bad behaviour at school, Kirsty wets the bed and they put that all on me… I started off like phoning the girls every week but that was too much for them, they were being naughty and they wanted to like leave a break in-between and I said well why don't we do it every four weeks? I wanted to phone them every day, all day but I done the best for them. If they ever needed me they could phone me…so that has worked for them.

Because of the concerns about the impact of the phone calls, telephone contact could also be 'supervised', which Lorraine objected to.

> I have to speak to the girls through a loud speaker so they can hear what I am saying to the kids which I think is out of order, I am their mother.

Where children had a history of getting upset and parents found phone calls difficult too, phone contact often was part of a briefer, more symbolic family arrangement. Joanne found it easier to have calls with fewer expectations and less pressure.

> I don't ring her anymore because she gets too upset… We like to phone her at Christmas and say Happy Christmas to her because it is a tradition we always used to have. And it gets a bit more

friendlier, so I have a word with her, everybody has a word with her, what did you get for Christmas you know, so she is getting used to that idea, but regularly no I don't.

Gaps in contact

Although there were no cases where it appeared a court order had allowed a local authority to refuse contact to the parents interviewed, there were examples where contact had simply stopped for periods of time when the child was in transition. It was unclear whether this was due to resource issues or was deliberate and for a reason, but the consequence for parents could be worrying.

> I don't know why – and that is like when Alistair went into care as well. They stopped contact for six months, because they were trying to transfer over social workers… And in that six months that is when he lost contact with me, because they stopped it deliberately. So when I saw him after six months he didn't even know who I was. (Judy)

Contact might be stopped when children moved to a new placement and this was said by social workers to be necessary so that the children could 'settle in', as described by Jenny.

> They just call it a three-month settling-in period, where they had moved the children there would be no contact in-between. I can't see that is a good enough reason, because after three months we are still going to be seeing them. If anything I think it would be better that you let the kids keep in contact with their parents, even though they are being shunted from pillar to post…

But not only was this gap hard for parents to understand, it seemed to result in some cases, as it did for Jenny, in longer periods of time without contact.

> My kids have been moved a couple of times since then and each time there is this settling-in period. I have gone nine months, ten months without contact because of social workers moving my kids to another foster carer, giving them a settling-in period.

Phone contact too could become seen as a threat to a new placement. So the principle of 'settling in' might be applied here too – as happened to Jenny. Delays in re-establishing phone contact made her feel powerless.

> We used to have regular phone contact and then when the girls moved and with the settling-in period it stopped. When we started saying like could we have phone contact again, they said oh we will sort it out, sort it out and then like social workers changed over again, do you know what I mean? And oh we will sort it, we will sort it and nothing ever gets sorted.

The general need for or benefit of a 'settling in' period are not supported by any research on contact, so for each child, foster family and birth family there would need to be a careful assessment of whether this was actually necessary or beneficial. Although there may be justification in some situations, perhaps where children's behaviour deteriorates after a phone call and new carers might struggle to cope, for some children moving between placements and having changes of social worker, the parent may be the most continuous person in their lives and may be able to help them 'settle in' to a new placement if handled constructively. Work with the parents may be more productive than breaking off contact if this actually adds to the child's anxiety at times of transition.

The value of contact

For all parents, the value of contact was about keeping in touch with children's lives, but children could also be active in this process.

> When Brendan is on holiday, he sends me cards and he sent me a postcard. He will buy me a present and that when he is on holiday. (Hannah)

Often this kind of contact sent powerful messages to the parents, and Hannah mentioned the special cards that Brendan sent to her and her partner.

> He sends me a Mother's Day card and he sends me birthday cards and like when it is Father's Day and that, he sent Eric a Father's Day card.

It was important for children to stay connected to what was going on in their birth families' lives. As described in Beek and Schofield (2004a), foster children still need to feel they have a special place, a niche, in the birth family, even when placements are long-term or when contact is infrequent. For the child to find or maintain this niche requires some exchange of information and sharing of experiences, as changes in the birth family occur. In this example, the child needed to make the acquaintance of the new family dog.

> We told Rhys during the last visit we had got a dog and he wanted to meet the dog. So I took her on the playground. He was throwing the ball for her and she loved it. (Gina)

Notice here that the news of the dog and the planned meeting provides a reason for parents and children to anticipate the contact with pleasure, allows the child to picture his parents having the dog to look after now – but also the dog then rewards the parents and the boy by loving the game and confirms the boy's place as 'family'.

For a child to participate in the key rituals of family life can sometimes be significant and can define the child's role in a family. As Beek and Schofield (2004a) found, being involved with a foster-family bereavement could help to seal the child's bonds with the foster carers, just as being involved with a birth family bereavement can help the child continue to feel still part of *that* family.

> Carly did come down because granddad died. She wanted to come and see Nana. Nana didn't really want her about, but she couldn't say no. Carly just wanted to be comforting to mum and they (social services) said I could go round for a couple of hours. Me and Barry took her for a walk so mum could be left alone for about half an hour to herself... We went round where Carly's granddad used to take her. She said, 'We went the granddad walk'. Then we had the funeral, which she come down for. (Joanne)

This child had extra reason to come to see her family at this time, and it proved that she still had a place in this family, and shared the family stories, 'the granddad walk'. The grandmother perhaps felt she could not refuse, so the mother has to manage the situation, the emotions of both her mother and her child, with the help of her partner. Even in this situation the mother needs permission to take her child for a walk. This particular child was very happily absorbed into her foster family, but nevertheless wanted to give and to get support as part of the ritual of birth family grieving. When we think of the principles of life story work in terms of constructing a coherent narrative of the child's place in both foster and birth families (Schofield and Beek

2006), it is easy to see why events such as these that become part of the shared memories of both the parents and the children are valuable. Foster families will need to be reassured that this need not detract from foster family membership and social workers need to be clear that membership of both families can, for some children, be conducted in parallel family networks.

This principle of parallel, but interlocking, family networks was important for managing contact around all kinds of family events. Several parents when talking about the reality of their loss of normal family life when children came into care (as discussed in the previous chapter) emphasised the loss of traditional family celebrations. For some parents, therefore, the arrangements for contact at key family times, such as Christmas, were especially significant. Where contact arrangements worked well, there might be a sense of shared parenting between carers and parents, more like that between collaborative resident and non-resident parents in divorce, including the expectation that older children might make their own decisions. In this probably rather unusual case, Karen described how the children alternated Christmas between the birth family and the foster family.

> Christmas time they came on the 24th and I had them until the 27th – so that was a really nice year. It is the first Christmas that I have had them actually overnight since they have been in foster care. The year before that I had them the 23rd to the 24th and so we give them their presents a day early. Then they said the next Christmas it won't be a long visit they will be with the foster carers. They are going to do it like every other year I will have a long visit. But Conrad (oldest child) he can either stay at his foster carers' or he can choose to come here, so they give him the choice as to what to do.

Because there was a high investment by parents (and no doubt children) in these contacts on special occasions, there could be corresponding lows when arrangements did not work out. Even with an active parent like Karen trying to check in advance, travel arrangements for a special family occasion broke down and the feeling of disappointment was acute.

> I was supposed to have Isabel and Joe for a day visit and Conrad was here then and it was my birthday. We arranged for a BBQ on Saturday and it was a lovely day, it was quite warm and that.

> The social worker said 'I will sort out the transport' but they didn't come. Apparently something had happened, she had been off for a couple of week. I tried to phone her that week to see if they were coming but she weren't at work at the time you know so they didn't come on the Saturday and I was really upset because obviously Conrad won't see them now until September time.

Because family contact in this case was complicated, involved more than one foster family and took significant resources it was not always possible to make up for missed occasions. So long gaps could occur. But each disappointment was a reminder that they were in a relatively powerless position as parents – and children were similarly dependent on social work staff to make contact plans work.

Some parents tried to help their children manage the intervals between contact visits. This mother used a doll to try and maintain her presence in the child's mind during her lengthy prison sentence, but also so that the child could take comfort from the doll in the absence of her mother.

> In one of the prisons I made her a rag doll Lulu and I dressed her and everything, I really wanted to keep it myself when I finished it! But I gave it to Jessica and as I was giving it to her I think Jessica was about four then I kissed Lulu and when I gave it to her I said, mummy has put a kiss there whenever you want a kiss from mummy kiss Lulu and that is a kiss from mummy. And even now Jessica is ten, she stills says she kisses Lulu because she knows that mummy kissed her and she can get a kiss from me. So you know it is just small things and I mean that must be what six years ago and she has still got her. (Amy)

Parents' own emotions around contact were hard to deal with. However much they valued contact and tried to find ways of thinking positively about it over the years, it was still hard.

> I do find them a little easier, yes. It is still emotional obviously because I have to say 'goodbye' again but it is not as emotional because it is not all six kids they're crying and you know what I mean, it is not so hard. But yes it is still very emotional, still very hard. (Eddie)

There were times when parents wondered if contact was worth the distress to children and to them.

> Well I suppose yes because we only get to see each other three times a year so it is very intense when you get to see each other and I suppose all the feelings come flooding back do you know what I mean. They want to come home and I do actually find the visits sometimes can be quite disruptive for everybody you know. Sometimes I have even got to the stage now where I have started thinking to myself that I am just better off staying the hell out of the way you know because I do, I just sometimes feel it is so damn disruptive for them and me. (Eddie)

After contact visits, his wife knew to leave him to process all the feelings.

> But when he gets back I know it is best just to leave him alone and he'll tell me what I want to know later on or the next day because he is trying to work it all out in his head exactly what they have said and everything so I just let him have a bit of head space first before we talk about the visit. (Denise)

Conclusion

As this chapter has shown, it continues to be very hard to get contact right for everyone. A small number of parents who were very resolved about their children being in care, and who have relatively relaxed relationships with social workers and carers, seem to have found arrangements that work for them. At the other extreme, for some parents, no arrangements could help them get past the general sense of anger and loss. But for most parents of children in foster care, as for non-resident parents after divorce, contact may have its difficulties but these had to be faced and got round if their relationships with their children were to survive. Sorting out the difficulties and ensuring that contact was reasonably enjoyable and constructive, however, did rely on relationships with foster carers and social workers – and these are explored in the next two chapters.

Contact: key themes and implications for practice

- The factors that affect parents' experience of contact with their children in foster care (e.g. frequency, venue, supervision) have particular but changing meanings in long-term placements as children get older and parents' attitudes change.

- The goal of contact is no longer assessment or reunification, but 'simply' maintaining a relationship over the years of separation. The quality of the parents' experience of contact is likely to be key to their ability to maintain a meaningful and comfortable role as parents. On the other hand, the way in which parents view their role as parents of children in care will also be affecting the quality of contact for them and for their children.

- Feelings of powerlessness in relation to contact are common among parents; although some parents do say that they are actively consulted about contact, while other parents have argued for and obtained changes in arrangements.

- Often parents' concerns are about whether arrangements enable children to enjoy contact, because if not, they as parents will be less likely to enjoy it.

- Managing contact with groups of siblings creates dilemmas for parents as it does for children, carers and social workers. Parents wish to see children together, but their need for 'quality time' with each child may not be compatible. Also, children may have reacted very differently to their early experiences and to being in care, so their ability to sustain contact with siblings and parents together needs very careful assessment and review.

- The growing use of different forms of communication, such as mobile phones, email and social networking sites, has created a much more complex picture regarding the planning, support and regulation of contact between parents and foster children. Although this is true for all children in care, for children where the permanence plan was for children to become full members of foster families, there may be additional tensions if parents and their children have almost constant access to each other and parents do not support the placement.

6.

Parents' Relationships with Foster Carers

For parents, the relationship with foster carers is inevitably going to be a testing one: testing in particular their ability to accept the role that foster carers are playing in their children's lives, regardless of whether parents accept that the children should be in care.

As the previous chapters have described, parents' feelings about the child being in care, about the placement and about contact were very varied and depended on a range of factors, from how well the child was doing to what parents felt about the reasons for care. The nature of the relationship between parents and carers was therefore going to relate very closely to the themes discussed in the previous two chapters, since the parents' ability to be supportive of their children growing up and thriving in foster care and their satisfaction with the quality of contact with their children would both have an impact on their attitude to foster carers and willingness to engage with them. On the other hand, the foster carers' attitudes and approach as experienced by parents would also have a big part to play. In this chapter we focus on the attitudes and ideas that parents held about carers and in particular the relationship between parents, who were no longer daily caregivers for their children, and foster carers, the daily caregivers who had been given, in many respects, the role of parents.

Perhaps one of the most surprising features of the accounts we heard was how little contact many parents had with carers. Very few parents saw carers at all regularly or spoke to them on the phone. The most common experience was probably to have met the carers at an early stage in the placement, but then if parents were not invited to attend LAC reviews, often held in the carer's home (a possible reason for not being invited), and contact was managed by social workers or contact supervisors, there would be no reason or opportunity for parents to have any communication with foster carers.

Nonetheless, it is important to analyse both the more and the less active relationships that did exist, as well as the ideas that parents had about the carers and what they thought carers thought of them. These ideas were often preoccupying parents, would affect their feelings about the child's placement and about themselves, and could be communicated to the child during contact. Some of the ideas from this and the previous chapter will be further developed in Chapter 8 when we consider how parents currently felt about their identity as parents, a theme which emerges here when discussing whether foster carers could be seen as 'real parents'.

As this relationship between parents and carers is discussed, very different pictures and questions emerge about what is expected of this relationship. In particular, questions arise about whether the factors that make the relationship more or less constructive for everybody, including the child, are linked to the social workers' (and maybe the carers') expectations of 'permanence' in the placement. If what is expected of the foster placement is a family that is more committed, more like a 'real family' or even a 'forever family', does this appear to require or encourage carers to be more exclusive of the birth family? Carers are often blamed by parents when this exclusivity occurs, but there are important questions to be asked as to whether carers may be getting contradictory messages from social workers and care plans about valuing the child's birth family and yet keeping them at a distance.

Contact with carers – first meeting and the early days of a placement

The knowledge that other people, other parents, will be looking after your children, in their homes and as part of their family, is in itself a difficult idea to accept. Even the basic principle, the fact that these other people have been judged competent to look after your children where you have not is difficult. So the question of who these people are, what they look like, whether they are different from you, whether the children will like them or be happy with them – or even prefer them to you – are very important. Thus for parents to meet foster carers at an early stage is necessary and valuable; indeed it is essential. At the least that meeting helps to avoid too much fantasising about each other and, at best, may develop into a positive experience that builds a relationship and helps acceptance of the placement.

So tell me about the foster family Martin is with now? Have you met them?

Graham and Miriam, yes I have met them, they are a lovely couple. They are a beautiful couple… They are very kind people, they are.

So has that made a difference?

They are very nice people and as long as they are looking after my son that's all that matters. (Barbara)

Although one might think it was expected practice for parents and carers to meet at least once, this was not automatic, even where children moved on to permanent carers.

I was supposed to be meeting up with this foster carer and the only opportunity I got to see her was in a meeting, an hour in a meeting with a few other people and that was it and then she went. (Paula)

Several parents had not met the carers – or had perhaps met a female carer but not their partner. Gemma described taking the initiative to meet her son's new carer at contact.

When we first went to contact, the first time, I saw this woman dropping Kelvin off, and she went to walk away and Jean, the social worker, said, 'See you later Esther', and I went, 'Hang on a minute is that his foster mother?' and she went 'Yeah' and I went 'Well I want to go and talk to her' and Jean didn't seem too keen about it. But me and Esther hit it off straightaway and I said, 'You know they would have had you just drop him off and not say a word to me?' and she said 'No I wanted to talk to you, but I didn't think I was allowed.' So I took the ball in my own court and said, 'No I am going to speak to her', and I remember running after her as she went to her car.

This scene is hard to imagine – it is as if the mother is invisible or would not be expected to take an interest in meeting the person caring for her son, or indeed that the carer would not wish to meet the mother. It is perhaps more likely that in practice a general concern that a mother might cause trouble and upset the child or the carer would be a factor that kept mother and carer apart. In this particular case, the snatched meeting with the carer did not lead to regular contact between the parent and the carer, but it did leave the door open and enabled Gemma to feel less anxious about her son over time. And the significance of simply being able to picture and have some sense of the person who is caring for, mothering, your son is undeniable.

> No I don't speak to Esther often, but I see her when she brings the kids to visits. Just lately, because the visits aren't held near her home anymore, she hasn't been bringing him. But I know if ever I was worried about anything I could write her a letter.

When parents were invited to reflect on their first meeting or early contacts with the child's carers, it was often a defining memory for their loss of the child and the transition away from full parenthood. For some parents, the meeting was important but the memory was of anger.

What was it like meeting the foster carer?

> Horrible. I was really angry as well and they said, 'She will be the one looking after your children'. And I thought, what gives them the right really? (Annette)

But for other parents, such memories of the early days also marked the beginning of a journey from focussing on their own feelings of anger and loss to focussing on the child's needs.

> I had a few arguments with Deirdre (carer), a few disagreements, because she had my children and I hated her for that, do you know what I mean? It was so difficult for me to go down there and see somebody else love my kids, you know? It fills me up (cries)... But Don and Deirdre are wonderful people, really, really nice people. We have a good relationship, you know. I said, 'If I can't get my kids back, please will you adopt them?' (Helen)

This mother was able to change her mind and demonstrated how some parents who cannot care safely for their children or meet their needs can nevertheless form a rapport with carers, such that they can accept that children are thriving and so want the children to stay in that family. As discussed in previous chapters, this acceptance of the placement is likely to help the child to settle, but does depend on some kind of developing relationship and respect for the carers, which usually suggests some degree of openness in the carers towards the parents.

Different relationships with carers who are open and inclusive or closed and exclusive

The ideal relationship with carers, according to the parents, seemed to be built on a combination of personal liking for the carer, recognition of the carer as caring well for the child and an easy, relaxed rapport between parent and carer. What was most important and valued was where the parent could ring the carer for information, which Louise found helpful in making contact a success.

> I phone Anthea and I ask her various questions about Ella, and what doesn't she like, so that I can bring her something, a little peace offering, a little icebreaker.

Louise's use of the terms 'peace offering' and 'icebreaker' indicates why it is helpful to have the preparatory phone call first. Louise could ring both her children's carers.

> And the same with Adrian's carer. I can ring them up and ask how my children are, and if I have got any concerns, how they are doing at school, you know.

Gina had been angry and upset about the process by which her son came into care, but her praise of his open and inclusive carer is fulsome.

> Andrea is a diamond – she has got Rhys. She is an absolutely lovely lady. She is like an old age pensioner, bless her! She will probably kill me for saying that, but she is an absolute diamond, she really, really is, she is absolutely fantastic. I mean she will talk to me, she never misses a visit, she will walk him down during the holidays and stuff and we get to see him in the school holidays and she can natter for Britain. She is so nice. I am so at ease with her. I think I could tell her anything. I feel as though I have known her for years.

Gina's appreciation of this carer was at least in part because the carer made it possible for her to be more involved with the child. She was clear about the difference between these carers and the carers for her daughters, who, she felt, seemed to exclude her from their lives. Such differences may be due to differences in the foster carers, as this parent suggests, but may also emerge when there are differences in the children's feelings for the parent or in the plan for the children in terms of frequency of contact or even simply difference in the age and stage of the child. Often carers were held responsible by parents, and could be given credit or blamed for aspects of the situation that may well have been due to factors beyond the carers' control.

Where there was a difference in relationship with carers of different children in a sibling group, and perhaps a more distant relationship with one than another, this was not always a barrier to appreciating what the apparently more distant carer did for the child.

> Elliot's carer and Kelvin's carer they are pretty down to earth, they are really nice to us. Alexis's carer I have only met her twice. I mean she wouldn't be my type of person but she is good to Alexis. (Tina)

Often the simple opportunity for parents to meet up informally with carers was rare but important.

> Jane when she brought him or picked him up she would come in for coffee and cake and everything and she would tell me how he is getting on and things. I've had really, really good contact with Jane. (Karen)

Carers were often older than the parents and where close and valued relationships developed, parents might see carers as parenting them too.

> Bridget is lovely. I couldn't wish for a better carer. Absolutely fantastic woman. We get on great. She is really like my second mum in some respects…she came to our wedding. She is bubbly, will talk to anyone. I do a lot of cross-stitch and Bridget frames them all, puts them up. (Kathy)

This carer, Bridget, was there for key rituals in Kathy's life, such as her wedding, but also marks her achievements. Building the mother's self-esteem in this way and including her in the foster family life and home made this, and other placements, at times feel more like an extended family placement. This will only be possible in certain circumstances, but can work well – and need not be a barrier to the child's inclusion in the foster family as a 'permanent' placement.

Although closeness and informality was possible in some cases, much of the contact and relationship between most parents and carers was regulated and restricted. In some cases this may well be necessary, but there were a number of cases where carers took the initiative to be more inclusive and empowering of parents. This may mean carers asking formal permission from social workers or an Independent Reviewing Officer (IRO) for specific events, but at times a telephone call is all it takes.

> Joan (carer) will say that there is a parents' evening coming up and things like that and Mandy (IRO) will say well could Karen (Mother) come along to it as well?... It doesn't always have to go through a meeting – sometimes Joan will phone me up you know, she is a hairdresser and obviously Isabel is growing up and she wants her hair in different styles or highlights and something in her hair or perming her hair and Joan will ask me first before she actually goes and does it – 'Is it alright if I do this with Isabel's hair?'.

In contrast there can be a lack of trust that develops between parents and carers, probably on both sides, which results in parents feeling and probably being excluded.

> I want to go to my daughter's review because I want to know how she is getting on at school. I want to be there to hear everything what goes on and I want to challenge them carers because I do not trust either of them. Them two ain't trying to like me. They have sort of got my daughter's mind so instilled with what they want to say they don't, I think, they don't want me connected with her. They want me cut out of her life.

It is difficult to know whether there was any room for negotiation to build trust in this relationship. The mother was very angry and unresolved and this may have meant that she did present some risk to the child's well-being in the placement. On the other hand, carers may have needed some help to work with the mother to reduce the antagonism. However, formal LAC review meetings where teachers and other professionals are present, in the foster carers' home, with the child often present too, would almost certainly not have been helpful in improving this relationship. Yet we rarely heard of attempts to sit parents and carers down together away from procedural constraints and contact in order to mediate and see if middle ground could be found.

Gina's experience, discussed above, of having very different relationships with carers of different children in a sibling group was quite common. Such differences may stem from different prior relationships between parent and child, different children, different carers and different social workers, who may promote or limit the degree of inclusion/exclusion in a placement. Sometimes parents felt that meetings were secretive to protect the carers and that they wanted and needed the direct communication that only carers can provide; for example, to get feedback on the children's feelings after contact. One mother believed that carers for two of her children were unwilling to be open with parents.

> The carers just don't want to involve me. They are my kids but they do not want me involved. They have to tell me if the boys are doing something because I am their mother. But if there weren't social workers and they didn't have to tell me they wouldn't... I would like them to involve me more. I would like to go to the meetings. I don't know if they have got something to hide, like not something to hide, maybe they don't want me to know exactly where they live and how they live and you know maybe they think that is not my prerogative to go into their house you know for these meetings or whatever... But after contact I would like to know about them, you know, not by a social worker – I would like to know from them.

As discussed in the chapter on contact, these situations of conflict must often leave the children in the most fraught family and placement situations having contact with unresolved, angry and anxious parents and living with carers who, for whatever reasons, are not communicating with the parents. Thus without intervention from the social worker to mediate the situation and do work with the child, the carers and the parents, children have to carry the burden of the antagonism and lack of trust that may have emerged between the two sets of parents.

Differences in relationships with carers who are 'down to earth' or 'superior'

Alongside and often linked to the extent to which parents might find carers inclusive or exclusive, parents found carers with an easy, accepting manner were more approachable and less likely to look down on them. The idea that carers might feel superior to parents was often a criticism that was made, with corresponding praise for carers who were more 'down to earth'. This is one positive description of meeting 'fantastic' carers at the carers' home.

> The place was lovely, absolutely lovely. Bernice and Fred are fantastic people.

What was it that made them fantastic?

> They were really down to earth. Very nice, they were very nice outgoing people to meet. Very friendly, easy to get along with, you could talk to Bernice. She is just one of these people that you feel you can talk to about anything. (Darren)

Parents valued carers who were down to earth, not only for themselves, but for their children.

> They live in a house out in the suburbs. I think they are great role models, because Will is really down to earth and likes his football and Martha is quite professional, quiet. You know they complement each other and I am happy with the role model Will gives to my son. (Louise)

The wish to be able to talk with carers in an easy way was common, but some parents felt it was not possible to relax because they felt carers were or saw themselves as 'above' them. As with inclusive/ exclusive approaches, this dimension could vary between carers for different children in a sibling group.

> I don't know how to put it, Joe and Isabel's carers are not sort of down to earth like me, they, oh they are quite, not posh but I think they think they are above me if you know what I mean?

Where does that impression come from?

> I just think obviously they think they are better than me. I think they think I should be praising them because they are looking after my children or something like that. That is how they come across to me, do you know what I mean? It is hard to say really.

And how about Conrad's foster carers?

> Oh no, they are brilliant they are, they are the sort of people that you can spend the day with and feel relaxed. (Karen)

One anxiety for parents was that not only did they think that carers were feeling 'above' them, but that carers may have said negative things to the children as a result.

> I believe because of the things they may have been told when they first got there, do you know what I mean? 'Oh your mum is a junkie, they didn't care about you.'

Parents could understand why carers might be negative about them, when they only had the official file reports to go on. However, it was still hard to be treated like the person in the reports.

> I have had carers that have just read a report on me. If you read a report on me, even if I read a report on me, it is like, what?! It is just black and white words to describe you, you know. This woman who was just hopelessly addicted to drugs, and lost her children, and did lots of time in prison. You know, certain people have got an opinion about that. But there were a couple of carers who were very bitter towards me, because they made it clear, you know, what they thought of me. (Louise)

Understanding where carers' critical attitudes came from did not make them any easier to deal with, especially when children might witness the way carers felt about or treated their parents. At times, the parents explained this problem in terms of the carers' very different life experiences, which dictated how they saw and felt about certain parents.

> Alexis's one is a bit snooty. I don't mean snooty, but what it is, she is a country girl, she has been brought up in the country. We are probably the first drug addicts she has ever laid eyes on and when I went to kiss her on the cheek at one of the visits she sort of looked mortified. I was just trying to say thank you. Well Dylan (son) said when I turned away, he said, 'God, if looks could kill, mum, you would have been dead!' But she is good to Alexis, so what else can I do? (Tina)

Parents' co-operation with carers is good for children

Co-operation with carers was sometimes seen by parents as giving important signals to children. Tina was not only able to understand and make allowances for carers' attitudes and behaviour, she was able to see the importance of remaining positive about the carers in front of the children.

> But I always say to the children at the meetings, you know, 'Say hello to your foster parents from us', and I am allowed to write to them both and I always put in the letters 'How are your foster parents?' So I have been supportive with their placements, right from the start... I never run down their foster parents or anything like that. In fact I have got quite friendly with one foster mother and I think that is better for the kids, because if I say 'Your foster mum is this and your foster mum is that' it would turn their minds wouldn't it?

As well as the benefit to the children of seeing her good relationship with the carers, Tina recognises that the carers have done a good job when she could not.

> I have always been nice about the foster parents, because as far as I am concerned they are bringing up my kids for me and the kids don't want for nothing, not now.

The supportive approach that Tina took to her children's placement was echoed in the accounts of other parents, who made sure that they were co-operative in ways that were a direct communication to the children.

> I think if the mother has a good relationship with the foster carers then the child will pick up on it – 'Well my mum is getting on with the foster carers so they can't be all that bad'. (Sophie)

> I know it is better for my children if they see the foster carers and their mum actually getting along without any dynamics of any kind. I have stopped doing that, it is much easier for me not to bring my silly resentments and inadequacies along to a contact so I don't. (Louise)

As well as giving positive messages to children, co-operative relationships between parents and carers could be a way of working together to ensure the well-being of the child. Alliances could be formed, both to help the child and to avoid the child manipulating the two-parent situation, setting carer and parent against each other.

> I wouldn't talk to Andrea (carer) about Jake with him in the room, so I will wait until he is at school and then I will phone her up and then I will tell her what is going on so she can sort it out her end. But then she has still got my, not my permission, but my backup because he turns us against each other. He asks Andrea

> for something and if she says no he says to me 'Andrea won't do this' or 'Andrea won't get me this and 'If I was at home you would…' because he is trying to turn, he is working one off the other. (Lorraine)

This kind of shared parenting needed good communication and willingness to trust on both sides, and was negotiated in ways that sounded similar to negotiations between resident and non-resident parents in divorce. But it also allowed parents to feel that they were putting the child first – even when this meant relinquishing extra parenting roles to the carers.

> I find sometimes that it is really difficult for foster carers, because if there is a major emergency and Ian has maybe fallen out of a tree and got a twig stuck in him, and he has to have an operation, they can't do nothing until they have got hold of us. Now if they can't get hold of us it means he can't have the operation. But as I said to them, if it is necessary for him to have it you do it and I will face the consequences afterwards because I have told you. And she went OK, we will do that.

This position was perhaps easier for Gemma to adopt because she was genuinely pleased with the care given to her children, but also because she was bringing up a subsequent child. This more successful parenting experience was raising her self-esteem as a mother and although not reducing her investment in the children in foster care, which was high, it allowed her to accept a shared parenting arrangement.

Chantelle, who grew up in foster care herself, was both consciously trying to support the foster carer in a co-operative way, while simultaneously defending her own role as mother.

> Right now I am trying to show my children that I care for them. I know they are where they are, but I have to keep showing my kids I love them, I respect them, I care for them. I am the same mum that was at home, feeding and clothing them and buying them everything. I need that balance for me and I need to keep a balance for the children. OK, I just ask the foster mum every so often, because I don't like to step on her toes in the way she does things. She is the foster mum.

There were also several examples where parents, the child and the foster carers formed an alliance to demand from the local authority what they both thought was right for the child, in one case both a school placement and an out-of-school activity. The carers also gave the child a role in asking for what he wanted.

> Gloria and Andy helped him chose a solicitor. They helped him go to the newspapers to get the right school because that is what he wanted to do. They helped him do Army Cadets, because that is what he wanted to do. They just got him the phone number and gave it to Ian and said right you want to do it you have got to do it, we can't do it for you. So he done that. (Gemma)

Although most of the co-operative relationships or alliances between parents and carers were based on shared positive attitudes to the child, they could be based on a shared negative view of child (see also Beek and Schofield 2004a). Darren, for example, was angry at his daughter for her difficult behaviour and was empathic for the carers when they ended the placement. If a close working relationship between parents and carers is based on blame of the child this can reduce the child's self-esteem further and leave the child feeling excluded and helpless.

Disagreements with carers – parents' anger

Parents who tended to be angry about their situation were also, not surprisingly, parents who were less likely to have constructive relationships with carers and less direct contact with the carers. Parents who wanted to maximise their involvement in their children's lives, but who were not able to let go of their right to make decisions for their children and who were making it difficult for carers, were often going to be, paradoxically, at risk of being allowed less involvement. If parents felt both angry and concerned that children were not in the right placement or that decisions were being made without consultation, this could fuel anger and upset in a vicious circle that might provoke restrictions and leave them feeling marginalised.

In this parent's account, the dispute focused on haircuts, often the source of disputes for parents of children in care, perhaps because changing how the child looks may appear to be changing the child's identity. In this case, Lorraine believed that the hair style selected by the carer was also against the wishes of the child.

> They (carers) told Sabrina that she had got to have a bob. Sabrina wanted her long hair but she had to have a bob, you know, she had to have her haircut. But I didn't get told about that either, they

just gone and done it. I am their mother, I should get asked. You
know every time I see my kids there is something different about
them.

Disagreements could also break out over differing ideas of appropriate
behaviour between parents and children. Some mothers, for example,
felt that it was right for a mother to kiss a child on the lips. Helen was
angry when this was not allowed at contact, because it was said to be
sexual. For Lorraine, the disagreement about kissing on the lips was
associated with a battle with the carer over her status as a mother.

> Sabrina wanted to give me a kiss, she jumped up and give me
> a cuddle and she wanted to give me a kiss. She went hang on a
> minute, she jumped down, she said to the foster carer she said,
> 'My mum wants a kiss. Where shall I kiss her?' He said, 'You kiss
> her on the cheek' and I said, 'No you kiss me on the lips, I am
> your mummy, kiss me on the lips'.

Conclusion

The question of how parents feel towards and relate to foster carers
is going to be a key element in how parents feel about the child and
the placement, as well as about their role as parents. The parents'
experience of carers as being very varied in their approach to them
was echoed by social workers in the focus groups in this project. Many
factors might be playing a part in this relationship between parents
and carers – for example, the age of the child combined with flexibility
around contact would affect how much of a role parents may have. But
the wide range of attitudes and approaches of foster carers to parents
was also a key factor that suggested there is room for more active
practice to nurture this relationship where, as seems likely, there might
be some benefits for the children.

Parents' relationships with foster carers: key themes and implications for practice

- Foster carers have taken over the care of their children and
  might be expected to be the focus of parents' anger. But, on
  the whole, parents were likely to give credit to carers for the

care they provided, unless they felt that carers made it difficult for them to have at least some role in the lives of their children.

- Relationships between parents and foster carers ranged on a spectrum from mutual warmth, close co-operation and a degree of shared parenting to being very controlled, distant and, in some cases, hostile. Where parents were on this spectrum depended on a range of factors in the child, the carers, the parents and the social workers, but openness needed to be worked at.

- Parents were able to discriminate between carers on different dimensions, e.g. those who were experienced as open and inclusive or closed and exclusive, down to earth or superior, (as parents saw it) in their attitude to parents.

- Such distinctions were often most evident when parents had members of a sibling group in different placements and saw differences in how carers responded to them – often linked to the extent to which some carers were perceived by parents as wanting to 'claim' children as their own.

- Where close relationships developed, parents and carers at times formed alliances to advocate on behalf of the child with social services or education, and children could thereby benefit. Where parents and carers shared a negative view of the child, the alliance resulted in shared confirmation that the child was to blame for problems.

- What emerged from these varied stories was that there could be a real benefit for parents, for carers – and therefore for children – if there were more opportunities for the carers and the parents to meet informally away from the tight agenda and minuted environment of the statutory LAC review meetings.

- The parents' relationship with the carers will also depend on the way in which carers have been prepared, trained and supported by supervising social workers. The emphasis on children's social workers as mediators of the parents' role leaves out the significant part played by the social workers with responsibility for the carers in influencing the approach carers may take.

7.

Parents' Relationships with Social Workers

Social workers play many roles in the lives of children in foster care, and the relationships between parents and social workers reflect both those different roles and the varied characteristics of parents and social workers. But from the parents' point of view, what matters most is that the relationship with social workers is the main route by which they can stay in touch with their children or maintain a role, however significant or limited, as a parent.

Social work tasks with parents when children are growing up in foster care are diverse, but are likely to include: explaining the court process and the care plan to the parents when the placements became long-term or permanent; arranging and perhaps supervising contact; providing parents with information about the children; managing the parents' participation in the LAC review process; checking certain permissions (e.g. travel abroad) with parents; speaking to the child about the parents; and offering support to the parents. The parents' relationship with social workers once children are in foster care is likely to be in the context of previous multiple contacts with social workers when they had received support when there had been problems in their family and/or when they had been subject to child protection interventions and court proceedings.

This is an extensive list of potential points of engagement with social workers, but relationships will, for all parents, have been with multiple social workers – as children's cases moved between teams at different stages, as re-organisations moved social workers around or social workers moved on. Each parent would bring to these relationships their own personality, history and current sources of anger, grief, loss, stress, anxiety and, for some, a degree of relief and gratitude when children did well. Each social worker would also bring to this relationship their own personality, history and current sources of anger, grief, loss, stress, anxiety and varying degrees of professional satisfaction, depending on whether they felt they had been able to do a good job for the child and the parents. This latter point is important, because many of the issues that affect children and parents, such as availability of placements or resources for contact, will not be in the control of the social worker, yet the social worker will feel a sense of personal responsibility and may bear the brunt of everyone's feelings. (The social work experience will be further discussed in a later chapter.)

As with all aspects of parents' experience, their relationships with social workers were rarely simple, and this range and complexity was one of the most fascinating aspects of this research. The accounts given by each parent were not only different from each other's, but were rarely internally consistent. Just when it seemed that a parent could not get any angrier or more hostile about social workers, she or he might say, 'But there was that social worker that was lovely' or 'I couldn't want anything better for my children'. Similarly, in accounts by parents who were apparently highly accepting of the need for care and the importance of co-operation, a parent might suddenly say that of course the social worker should allow the children to come home tomorrow.

For this reason, this chapter will address themes rather than be structured around 'types' of parents. As will emerge, there were parents who were predominantly positive about social workers or predominantly negative, but that is never the whole story. So in building a picture that does justice to the complexity of their accounts, the chapter is structured around four themes that parents talked about most and which seemed to define their view of relationships with social workers: information and communication; involvement: negotiation and co-operation; being understood; and trust.

Information and communication

Given the range and significance of roles that social workers play in the lives of parents of children in foster care, it is not surprising that one of the keys to the quality of relationships was the quality of communication between social workers and parents. On this communication would depend whether information about the children that was available to parents was regular, up to date, detailed, and covered areas that mattered to parents. Important aspects of communication included both the ways in which social workers were conveying or not conveying information to parents, but also, not surprisingly, the extent to which social workers were seen to be *available* and *listening* to what parents had to say.

The significance for parents of information about their children should never be underestimated, at any stage in the placement. In the early days, information needs to include what having a child in foster care will mean for them as parents. A number of parents had fears that it would cut them out of the lives of their children entirely, as Kathy described.

> They don't explain properly that you still have parental rights. They don't explain properly that you still get contact; it is only really in extreme circumstances that you don't get contact with the children. None of that was ever explained to me.

Kathy later felt more positive about what social workers offer.

> Do you know what I would love to be now? A social worker, because I now know that they do try and help.

Once the children were in placement, it was important for parents to stay in close touch with social workers, so as not to miss important information. Deepak was appreciative of the role that certain social workers had played in his sons' lives.

> The social worker who is on at the moment, even Arjun's last social worker, they have both been very helpful.
>
> **And how important is that relationship with the social worker for you?**
>
> Well you know that is the only way I can know anything about my boys. I have to make sure, you know, I am always in contact with them. If they are making any changes I want to be told about them.

Information allows parents not only to be reassured about the welfare of the children, but also to know of any changes and developments in the child's life. It was hard otherwise to keep up to date with the child and with events in the child's life, which could make parents feel detached, irrelevant, excluded or disconnected. For parents who had been main carers, this dependence on the supply of information from the social worker was obviously a major change in how they connected with the child and their role. But even for separated fathers who had not previously been main carers, a lack of information could be frustrating and make it harder to sustain their identity, while a good supply could help them build a still limited but more satisfying role and relationship.

It was acknowledged by parents that social workers might be put off contacting them with information and keep their distance because of fears that parents would be hostile. As Sophie suggested, rather than letting this distance develop and persist, social workers should listen to parents more, so that relationships might improve.

> Most parents associate social services with people that take children away from parents and parents get hostile. But if social workers sit and listen to what the parents want and what they don't want and what help they can give them, maybe things would be a lot better.

Where practical help as well as advice was provided by social workers, parents felt that barriers had been reduced and someone was caring about them and trying to help.

> Yes they did help, they were brilliant, actually, they were excellent.
>
> **What made them excellent?**
>
> They were good if you can't get to places – they will pay your train fare and they will pick you up and make sure you get there and get back. They just advised you on the best possible way to cope with things and what is best for the children, you know, and where it is best for them to be and things like that. (Karen)

The parents' experience of the *availability* of social workers was, of course, very important for effective communication. Most parents had concerns about their children, concerns that were often well-founded. Although many children made good progress in foster care, they often continued to show difficult behaviours and signs of distress that needed to be addressed. Where the social worker was trusted to be available and was willing to contact parents as well as respond to their concerns, it helped parents to relax a little.

> Dena (social worker) is really good, I haven't got any faults with her.

What makes Dena good?

> I can talk to her and if anything ever happens she is straight on the phone to me, you know if they were ill or something had happened she says I will always let you know. You know I am a bit of a worrier, I talk to her on the phone about how I am feeling and she understands. (Annette)

This description of the attentiveness of the social worker is clearly experienced by the mother as part of a mutual and open relationship, which acknowledged their shared interest in and concern for the well-being of the child. It also suggests that the social worker was empathic and attentive to the emotional well-being of the mother and recognised that the mother could not manage her anxiety without the social worker's support.

The value of being given regular information was mentioned frequently by the full range of parents, from the most co-operative to the most hostile, but the lack of some important information was also reported. For all parents, not knowing where their children were, not knowing when the children moved placement or then not having the chance to meet new carers were particular sources of concern.

> I would like just regular updates and to have things explained. I can't believe I haven't been introduced to these new people who have got my eldest boy, I think it is terrible. (Philip)

Where social workers had not communicated information to parents promptly, it was sometimes the children who passed it on.

> If it wasn't for Callie telling me what was happening…she told me what day she was moving. I got a phone call from her social worker two weeks later to tell me that Callie had now moved in with her permanent foster carer. I went, well that is great, but that actually happened two weeks ago. (Jenna)

Although it is understandable that delays in communication can happen, this particular delay caused an alliance between parent and child based on criticism of the social worker. One of the inevitable practice dilemmas for social workers is how to communicate information not only promptly but also appropriately. So, for example, the opportunity to move a child to a new permanent placement, as in this case, might come up quickly, but if a social worker could not speak to the parent it would seem bad practice to maybe leave a message on an answer machine about something that needed proper explanation and discussion. Workers must always be weighing in the balance the relative benefits of speedy communication for the child over delayed but more appropriate communication for the parent.

Because of the potential number of people in the team around the placement (the child's social worker, the carer's social worker, the contact supervisor, the IRO, the various managers, social work assistants, students) who might pass on information about the child to parents, it is perhaps not surprising that at times wires get crossed and parents are left uncertain about what was really going on. Such problems were compounded when social workers changed.

> It seems like you will get one social worker who will tell you something about one of your kids or something that is coming up or something that has gone on. And you will sort of hear half a message or half a story and then you will get hold of somebody else who has actually been dealing with the kids who will come up with something completely different… Promises that they make you and things they tell you. Then when you actually go back to get these things instated and get them up and running, like they have said they are going to do, someone else has been put on the case and they turn round and say they didn't have no right to tell you that, this isn't going to happen, and you know it is all just…
>
> They have said they will do this and they are going to do that and they are going to look into this and they are going to look into that and the next thing you know, it either hasn't been done or they have left and they have got another social worker.

Frustrations were great when parents felt that they had done their best to communicate, but were told there was no record.

> They said that I haven't phoned up when I have, and I have phoned up and said I can't make this time because I am not very well or something has happened and I have been up all night and I am tired you know and people are saying that I haven't phoned up and I am thinking I can't win, I can't win with Social Services at all you know, my life has been turned upside down.

As this mother says, when communication does not work, parents are reminded of their overall sense of loss of control. Although again it is understandable that in big organisations it may be hard to keep track of messages and information, there is a significant impact on parents. The effort for parents in sustaining both a role in the child's life and a relationship with the social workers that made that parental role possible was rarely easy, but problems with communication made them feel all the more helpless.

As is already apparent, parents needed to hear information from practitioners, but also to be heard. Listening to parents was said to be important not only, as above, to relieve anxieties about the child or to keep a parent up to date with a placement move, but also because parents felt that they had information and views about their children that could be of benefit to them. Parents talked of being experts on their children and therefore well-placed to be an advocate for them. Gemma felt very strongly, from her knowledge of her son, Ian, that the most important thing for him was to stay with his current foster carer. She said she insisted on being heard.

> I said you take him out of them foster carers, I said, you are back to stage one. I said leave the foster carers. Change the social worker by all means and change the reviewing officer by all means, but do not change the foster carers because that won't help. They went right, OK. They got him a new school. They got him a new social worker. It took them ages, but they finally got a new reviewing officer. We walked into the meeting and she said right today is a new start; we don't talk about the past, we don't talk about the problems he has had in the past or anything, we talk about from here, day one. And Ian went 'YES!'

Ian had very challenging behaviour, but this placement went on to continue to be very supportive and successful during Ian's teenage years. As his mother's account shows, from the content and the tone, being listened to, when it contributed to action for the benefit of the child, could significantly boost the sense of being a good and actively involved parent.

Other parents felt their views were not taken into account enough. As this separated father, who described trying to alert children's services to the need to protect his daughter from her mother, suggested.

> I would say to a social worker, don't discount what the parents of that child say to you immediately. Think about what has been said, don't immediately ignore it. Then take into consideration that they might know a little bit more about the situation than you do. (Gerry)

Most people naturally tend to judge whether they have been listened to in any context on whether their views result in action. But these situations are not simple, and in Gerry's case it may have been that at the time the child expressed a strong wish to be with her mother and/or she had not done well in the past when in foster care *and* the father had not been willing to offer a home. Social workers will always have to balance carefully the information and opinions they receive from both parents as well as other sources when they try to determine the best option, or sometimes the least harmful option, for a child. But nevertheless it is important to take into account these experiences of parents who had felt somehow irrelevant to the process.

Involvement: negotiation and co-operation

There were clear links between the quality of the communication with social workers and the parents' wish to be involved to whatever degree was possible in their children's lives. Parents sought involvement because of the risk of losing touch with their children, which would create more problems, as this father suggested.

> I think social workers need to change the way they do things, because feeling entirely out of touch with your children is the worse thing that you could ever possibly do. They should make sure that the parents are involved in everything the children do and when they're not, that is when the problems start.

Again it is possible to hear the tensions that can arise over the expected role of parents for children in long-term placements. It was certainly possible in some cases for parents to work closely with social workers and be given a sense of involvement. Often it was not so much specific pieces of information that parents required to facilitate involvement, but a sense of open communication, so that the parents' wishes could be expressed and taken into account and they could act like parents.

> When Stefan (social worker) phones me up he asks when I want to see her. I am due to see her in October, but I am hoping it will be the end of October. So then I can phone Stefan up and ask what she wants to do for Halloween so that I can go out and buy her a Halloween costume, in case they are having parties. (Judy)

Judy, like parents in intact families, was watching through the year for the dates when children have special times or cultural rituals. Anticipating a child's life, keeping a child in mind in this way, needs support in terms of the social worker's availability and openness to give them information and make the relationships work. This kind of openness is not about increasing the amount of the parent's direct contact with the child, but more about making their parenting role more effective so that parents get parental satisfaction in the child's pleasure.

However, it is worth noting that although this example of communication, co-operation and parental involvement over Halloween sounds positive from the parent's point of view, the foster carers who have full-time care of the child and have been asked to integrate the child as a member of their family may also have wanted the pleasure of providing the child's costume or have felt that it was their role. Special occasions in particular can create dilemmas for carers and children as well as parents, but also for social workers. This tension may make workers inclined to withhold some information from parents to avoid potentially awkward rivalries between parents and carers for a role in the child's life and a place in their affections that may put pressure on the child to choose.

The movement of the child into more long-term arrangements where carers might play a different role was remarked on by most parents, with the first change being how the frequent and significant involvement before and during the court hearing fell off afterwards.

> Before we had to get all the health permissions but now we are not allowed to – it all changed after the court hearing. I don't feel like I am a part of their lives at all. I don't know about… I asked about dental appointments, I ask about eye appointments and I get nothing back from the social workers, so I don't feel I am a part of their lives at all.

This mother's feeling that her role in the children's lives had been changed and reduced does reflect an actual shift in parental roles and responsibilities that is intended in the making of a care order, when health appointments often become the responsibility of the foster carers. Parents may know about such appointments, but they are not involved. As this parent's account shows, however, the task of adapting to and coming to terms with this reduction in their role is not straightforward

Staying involved as parents could mean very different approaches to the relationship with social workers – for example, being active and assertive, or co-operative, or pushy and embattled. A dilemma for parents was often how to be active and assertive, how to get what you feel you want and is right for you and your child, without causing difficulties. For some parents, it took them a while before they felt able to be assertive and to state what they wanted. Karen began by advising other parents to 'speak out', but ended by expressing gratitude for the support of social workers, suggesting that these need not be incompatible.

> Some people don't like to speak out or some parents just carry on and do what the social workers say, you know. Whereas sometimes parents need to sort of speak out and say no, I don't want it like that, I want it like this, you know. I mean a few years ago, I would have just done that, you know. But now if I want something done, I will say, 'Can we do it like this instead of doing it like that?' I don't know really where I would be if it wasn't for social workers' support actually; they have done a brilliant job.

In this account, being assertive as a parent, saying what you think should happen, is seen as important, but not as negative or aggressive. Note that being assertive here is saying, 'Can we…?' and so suggests the opening of a negotiation rather than making a demand. But the outcome feels both empowering and supportive.

Being willing to negotiate was an important part of what was the beginnings of a co-operative relationship – though some parents' motivation to negotiate and co-operate was built on anxiety about the consequences if they did not.

> I have always co-operated with social services… Well I have heard stories where people have gone against social services and they have made it worse for themselves. I thought it might make it a bit easier for me, because you might as well work with them rather than go against them. So I do work with what they are saying to

> me. I don't always agree with what they are saying, but I just keep it to myself. (Joanne)

Most parents were aware that there was a plan for their child to remain in foster care and some said that they had always done things by the book for the sake of the child and to avoid disrupting this plan.

> I have done everything I have been told to do, I haven't rung when I am not supposed to ring, I have written when I am allowed. I am not allowed to ring anymore, but I have kept by the book. I have turned up to every appointment, you know.
>
> **What makes you still do it by the book, do everything that the social workers are saying?**
>
> Because I don't want to jeopardise their (the children's) plan, you know. Their father said in his court statement that he was driving past the house, to see if he can see them. I have never done that and I wouldn't do that simply because if I got caught, what if they took my kids from Deirdre and Don far, far away, it wouldn't be fair on them and they wouldn't settle with anybody else. If they took them away from Deirdre and Don now it would be like taking them away from me when they did and it wouldn't be fair and they wouldn't settle with anybody else and they are happy where they are. (Helen)

Again, however much this mother struggled with the fact that the children were in care, she was able to focus on the needs of her children and to appreciate the value of stability and continuity with the carers to whom the children were attached.

For some parents, it took a while before they had felt able to let go of some of the anger and be more co-operative. But as time went on, it can become possible to manage feelings if only because it made life easier for the parents if they could do so.

> So instead of me doing what I would normally do, which would be to kick off and be aggressive and be violent because I am not getting my own way, I am pretty much letting it wash over me. I know there is nothing I can do about it; it doesn't matter how much kicking and screaming, it is not actually going to change things. So there is no point in ruffling feathers in the meantime. It makes my life harder, you know, so I think people, well the authorities, are actually seeing a change in me as well. (Paula)

Moving from a position of anger and blame to one of co-operation with social workers was explicitly described by another mother. Louise showed considerable ability to reflect on relationships and her own development from a background of drug addiction, but also to be able to reflect on the feelings of the social worker.

> Me and Sally get on very well, you know we almost chat for hours.

> **OK, so is she quite approachable, can you ring her?**

> Yes absolutely, we have got a pretty good relationship like that.

> **What do you think it is that makes this relationship different from that with other social workers?**

> I think it has got a lot to do with my attitude as well; I stopped blaming the system and holding onto things that haven't gone so well, because I was really good at that, I was really good at saying, 'I told you this placement wasn't right, why am I not listened to?', 'I told you these people were going to reject my children', you know. I was bringing that sort of stuff and I still would, but not in that manner. I was quite sad and quite blaming.

> **What has happened in order for you to co-operate rather than to blame them?**

> Because the atmosphere is always very tense on visits, if you are in a situation where you are sitting with a social worker you have got a resentment with and blaming and she is probably a bit, you know, on tenterhooks because they can feel this. Then that reflects on the children and then the carers and it is just futile. I have just discovered it is futile. It is far easier to just go along and cajole, 'OK tell me what I need to do. I am not saying I agree with all of it, but tell me what I need to do…'

Managing feelings and co-operating with social workers for the sake of the children was mentioned by several parents, rather as they talked of the benefits to the children of seeing parents co-operating with foster carers. Co-operation with social workers in front of the child was deemed to be helpful.

> I want him to see us getting on rather than at each other's throats because that isn't going to do him any good. So me and Laura (social worker) on Monday we took a stroll, I had a right old gas

> with her, you know. Rhys can see that we get on and I think it helps him in the long run, knowing that me and Laura get on. I get on well with her. She is fantastic. (Gina)

This comfortable relationship was obviously comfortable for the parent and the social worker, and perhaps the fact that the parent could feel it was in the child's interests helped her to relax with the social worker.

Maintaining their confidence in the social worker and doing things by the book was easier when the children were settled and thriving, but harder at times when plans for the children appeared to drift or even stall.

> At the moment we are in limbo yes. You know the plans that were put in place, they were all going really well. And then all of a sudden we just came to a grinding halt, just for the sake of waiting to hear a few words from one person that just happened to go away on holiday, you know, that was really inconvenient. How dare he choose to go on a holiday? I don't care if he works hard all year, you don't go on holiday when we need you. So we are in limbo at the moment and there is not much we can do. But again hopefully in the next few weeks things should pick up from where they left off and we will be able to carry on moving forward.

The frustrations for parents in getting things done led to accounts that were less about co-operation and more about being persistent.

> You can't just sit. Like I will phone them and then expect them to get back. Then a couple of weeks pass and then you phone again and they are out of the office and before you know it a couple of months have gone past and I haven't had no contact. Yeah you have got to keep chasing them up.

Without a sense of involvement, parents felt they had to protest loudly, like this father:

> When people say you lose your kids, you do. You lose them completely and utterly. They go into the system and it is like they don't exist or it's like we don't exist. Unless you actually make a noise.

Maintaining the involvement and the role they wanted and felt entitled to led to some parents having a sense of *fighting* the system and the relationship becoming a battle.

Sometimes it is frustrating with social services that they don't want to involve you. You know I had to fight to get her school report or her school photograph, you shouldn't have to fight for those things, you know.

When it came to being involved, social workers might therefore be seen as friends and allies, or, at the other extreme, as enemies to be defeated. For most parents, where they were on this continuum varied depending very much on the interaction of different factors, such as the parents' degree of acceptance of care, the social worker's availability and approach, the stage in the placement and the state of the parents' own lives.

Being understood

Perhaps one of the most difficult issues for all parents who wanted to continue to be involved as parents in their children's lives was their need to feel understood. They wanted social workers to understand both their overall position, as parents who no longer have their children with them, and the impact on them, as individuals with feelings, of each contact, each review, each Christmas and each birthday – theirs and their children's. As the years went by, there were many times when parents had to manage difficult situations and difficult feelings, and when they wanted social services as an organisation and social workers as people to understand their position and their feelings. Being understood operates at both a cognitive and an emotional level. Parents wanted their difficult situation understood and appreciated, but also wanted evidence from social workers of empathy for their feelings as mothers and fathers who had not been able to bring up their children.

Even parents who were very positive about the carers struggled sometimes with the sense that the depths of their feelings were not fully understood by social workers.

I'm relieved and grateful to Bridget (carer). I can't say I am grateful to social services, but I know they have to do a job. I will say one thing about social services, they do a good job yes – just be more aware of parents' feelings, because we are human, we do hurt. (Kathy)

> If they can remember what the person is going through, losing their kids and the pain that that causes. We are not made of stone, none of us are made of stone. (Tina)

Many parents did not believe that social workers could understand them, because they were young or had not had children themselves. This was again in contrast to foster carers.

> Social workers have just got to be more understanding, if they haven't had kids. I think it is a case of sometimes they just don't understand where the parents are coming from, whereas the foster carers have actually had kids and they can understand where the parents are coming from. They understand all the stresses and everything but social workers don't. (Gemma)

Sometimes parents focussed on the difficulty for social workers who have had easy lives in understanding their own troubled lives.

> They couldn't basically understand my position, how vulnerable I was... Social workers go on text books they don't look at the overall picture, they don't look at reality, how people live, what their lives have been through. A lot of social workers they have had life easy, they have had loving parents, they have had a good education, they haven't had the raw deal. (Alison)

These differences in life experience and circumstances as perceived by parents will exist between many, though not all, social workers and parents, and they are not easy for either to manage comfortably and openly. Yet workers and parents need to work together to maintain a relationship, regardless of these differences, that functions well enough to support both the parents and the child. The capacity for empathy does not rely on social workers having had the same difficult experiences as the parents, but sometimes workers may need support at times to manage their own sense of privilege or having been lucky in life so that it does not get in the way of a relationship that can be helpful.

Trust

Any relationship needs a degree of trust in order to work. In this relationship between parents and social workers, the difficulty with achieving trust was often that most of the power was on one side.

From the parents' perspective, and in reality, the social work agency had most of the control over placement choice, contact arrangements, reviews and so on. Parents could sometimes make things more or less difficult for the social workers, foster carers and for the children, but on the whole they felt, and probably mainly were, unable to have much of a say in major decisions.

Where social workers were seen as available and responsive, understanding the parents and offering the information they needed, parents felt they could trust social workers and did not fear the power that social workers had. Even so, there was often some hesitation about making demands.

> I don't like to ask – she (social worker) said she is there if I need her and I can ring her up any time. She is really kind. She went bowling with us last week and joined in and that was quite fun. I can ring her at any time. But I said what has happened to the photos? Because the foster carer never sends me photos of the girls and she said she will have a word with her. If I have got any doubts or something has happened, you know, with the girls and they are worried about anything she will ring me and tell me and say Megan is worried about something that has happened. But they are coping really well and they have really adjusted and I am quite pleased. (Annette)

For parents who have some trust in social workers, the feeling of not being trusted in return with basic information was difficult. When Annette did get photos, identifying information about school was removed.

> I got some last week and they were quite nice ones. But some are like cut in half, because obviously they have been taken with somebody else, you are not allowed to know who they are and badges get scribbled off, what school they are at. You are not allowed to know, you know, because obviously I don't know everything. They have got to be very careful I know, but it is quite hurtful.

Annette may not know whether this was a general policy, or whether there was something in her particular case that had made this secrecy necessary, perhaps therefore something she could discuss or challenge.

Developing trust in any one social worker was inevitably affected by the experience of social workers changing.

I don't know how many I have been through since they have been away, five probably six for the older kids, you know –

And how does that feel?

It does my head in, especially when it is someone new every time. For the kids, it's hard, but for me I find it extremely hard because I start getting used to one of them and I start to try and build up a little bit of trust, then I start to think right OK they are trying, and they disappear on me or they let me down, do you know what I mean? (Eddy)

My kids have had numerous, at least four, social workers each, my boys and my girls, if not more and just as you get to know the one and you get like your regular contact and get the phone contacts and the longer contacts and whatever then there is another social worker, all they know is what they have read and that. (Karen)

These parents were positive about their current social workers, but changes that had happened in the past had made them lack trust in the stability and continuity of social workers.

One of the questions with new social workers was whether they would rely only on what was in the file. It is good social work practice to read the file, but the file may not always reflect how parents had moved on from the early, problem years. On the other hand, parents wanted social workers to read the whole file so that they could understand why the child's behaviour might be difficult.

I think there are far too many social workers and they are overrun by work and that is what I have noticed...some of them don't know any history they just get a report handed down from another social worker...sometimes I need to rein them in, say hold on a minute, maybe this child's behaviour has got something to do with, you know, this, that and the other. (Louise)

In some cases, social workers had changed, but reviewing officers had offered continuity.

Yes Mary has been the Reviewing Officer right from the beginning so of course I can talk to her and I get on really well with her. She is like a friend I suppose really now, yeah. (Gemma)

It was difficult for parents when their children became upset at the prospect of yet another new social worker, yet they could still appreciate, as could the children, when the new social worker was good.

> 'I keep having all these social workers and they keep leaving', Ian said, 'I have had enough!' And they went, 'Well, you are going to have a man' and he went, 'Right OK is he nice?' And they went, 'Yeah he is good' and Ian went 'Well I am not having him unless I meet him', so they said 'OK we will arrange it', so we met him and we got on really well.

Conclusion: what makes a good social worker from the parents' perspective?

The parents' view of what makes a good social worker included providing information and helping parents feel involved. But like most relationships with professionals of any discipline, what most parents wanted were people who were not only good at their job, but had personal qualities that helped parents relax, manage their feelings and find a role as parents.

> The social worker that Alice had she was fantastic, absolutely. She is the sort of person that social workers pretty much aspire to be like. She is approachable, she doesn't look down at you, she is on the level with you. You can talk to her almost like she is a friend; she is not an authority figure. She will tell you everything that is happening; she doesn't keep you in the dark. She keeps you posted, she keeps you updated. If she hasn't spoken to you for quite a while, just because nothing new is actually happening, she will phone you just to say, you know, I know nothing has been going on, but how have things been going and is there anything that you want? which was really good. She catered not just for Alice's needs, but sort of me and the others in the family as well.

Parents had no choice but to engage with social workers if they wanted to maintain a role in their children's lives, so they were grateful when social workers made that engagement not just bearable but actively helpful. What helped most from social workers was the recognition that for parents having your life and the lives of your children in the hands of others was not easy.

> It is just being able to be calm, tactful and very understanding that it is not your life, it is somebody else's life. (Chantelle)

Parents' relationships with social workers: key themes and implications for practice

- Issues of power and authority continue beyond the court and the care order, as the parent has to negotiate a role in a situation in which the local authority is the corporate parent, with the social worker as its representative.

- Given the potential for tensions in this relationship, it was encouraging to find a number of parents who were able to appreciate social workers who were efficient professionals who also understood their concerns at a personal level and did their best to help parents get the most from a difficult situation.

- Key to successful relationships in parents' eyes was the quality of the communication and involvement that social workers provided. This enabled them in important ways to retain a role as a parent, through knowing about the children's welfare.

- But parents also valued social workers who showed that they recognised the needs of parents as people, e.g. that the parent was especially anxious, or needed extra help to get the most from contact.

- Where problems arose for parents these were often linked with a lack of information and communication, which in turn was often linked to the lack of continuity of social workers. This pattern of change affected parents directly, but also affected the children in ways that made parents concerned and, at times, angry. When social workers changed, not only did the new social worker not always understand the situation fully, it also took time for parents to *trust* them.

- Perhaps what was most important was the simple fact that parents were not all, or always, hostile to social workers and could be very grateful and appreciative of help and support for themselves and their children.

8.

Am I Still a Parent? Managing a Threatened Identity

Key to this study was the parents' experience of the role of parent – given the loss of their children and the experience of their changed and dramatically reduced place in the lives of their children. As discussed in earlier chapters, there were tasks at the beginning of the process in coming to terms with loss and then in accepting the fact that the children were in care and living with a foster family. But over the years, as was clear from the parents' stories, there were further tasks to be faced in maintaining a sense of identity as a parent.

In this chapter we will explore some very different but linked aspects of this dilemma. First we will be considering what parents thought about the extent to which they still felt themselves to be parents, particularly in relation to the potential role of foster carers as parents. Then we focus on what we might learn from a very specific issue relating to parental identity – parents' views on whether it was OK or not OK for their children to call the foster carers 'mum and dad'. Finally, we will look more conceptually at the issue of the parents' 'threatened identity' (Breakwell 1986), as discussed in the introduction. Here it is possible to reflect on the strategies, sometimes explicit but more often implicit in previous chapters, that enable parents to manage the tension between the negative ways in which other people might see them and their wish to feel like, to be seen as and to be not only a parent, but also a *good* parent to their children.

Parents and carers – who are the real parents?

Parents had a trump card when it came to defining themselves as parents, which was biology. This did not mean that a biological mother could always fully identify herself in the role of mother for her child in foster care, but genetics helped.

Do you feel like Alice's mum?

Yes and no, yes and no. I mean I know she is mine. I mean she looks like me as well, which is something you can't get away from and she is so much like me as a person it is quite scary. (Paula)

Where children were well settled in foster care and parents were very accepting of the benefits of the care they received, parents could see the foster carers as able to meet children's need for a family, including providing key family members. This was normalising for the children and made it seem more like a real family experience.

I think now Ian has got used to the fact that he is disappointed that he isn't going to grow up with a dad. But I think he sees his foster carer, foster father, he calls him granddad because he is a granddad and he has been calling them nanny and granddad since day one. And I think that is good, because it means that with other kids that have got mums, dads, nans and granddads at least he has got them too. (Gemma)

In contrast, where children were seen by parents to be less well settled with foster carers, this could be attributed to a lack of the connection that a child would have with a 'real', biological parent and which later relationship building by foster carers could not replace.

Murray does have his off days: 'Mum I want to come down, I don't want to stay up here no more'. He will feel like that, because they aren't his parents, they didn't give birth to him and that. At the end of the day, they wasn't there when Murray was born. They have only bonded with him halfway through his life, but they weren't there from the beginning and they will never know what it was like.

This view reinforced this mother's own sense of being special to her son in a way that could not be replicated.

There were various ways in which the parents recognised that children might be torn between two sets of parents. Some saw this dilemma for the children, but concluded that, however much they were loved by the carers, given the choice, the children felt a stronger tie to them rather than the carers.

> They (the carers) have a genuine love for Joey you know they do, I can honestly say they really love him.

> **How does he feel about them?**

> I think he likes them, you know, but I know Joey, he wants to come back home with me. He loves his mum you know, he wants to come back home, but I know he doesn't want to be disloyal to Gail and Bill. He loves Gail and Bill, but at the end of the day I am his mum.

Parents' sense of the children's longing to be with them could be a source of reassurance of their value as parents, but could also be a source of sadness on the children's behalf. The parents had lost the children, but the children had lost the chance to have the normal experience of being brought up by their parents. This meant that parents had to find ways to signal that their real parents did still care about them.

> I feel sorry for the children, you know, because I know they are being looked after, but I just think it is not the same as having your real mum.

> **And what do you do to show them that you are still their mum?**

> I show them in my letters and say I hope you are OK, mum loves you lots and tell them what I have been doing you know. They love the cats and I say I have got three, Paddy, Leo and Pepsi. I say how they are and I send them photos. I am allowed to do that. (Annette)

Their sense that children did not have the usual experience of living with their real parents led to certain kinds of compensatory activities and communications. For Annette, sharing what she was doing and keeping herself alive in her children's minds as their real mum was the best way of making up for what she felt to be a gap in her children's lives. Quite a number of parents had pets at home and the messages to the children about them were often apparently simple and yet complex and ambiguous – as here. Annette's children did not have contact at home and see these cats, but it seemed that knowing about the cats might on the one hand reassure the children that their mum is OK and has some company and something to look after, while on the other hand may signal a cosy family home to which they could return, and also a safe home to which there was no reason not to return. These communications are always within the limitations of what is 'allowed', as this mother points out, and it would be hard to object to such letters. Yet children may need help in managing the range of more difficult thoughts and feelings that result from these communications.

One of the more common themes among parents who expressed concerns was that whatever happened, a foster home was not a real home. Parents expressed this view both from their own experiences of being in care and their perception of how children were experiencing the foster home.

> I know the foster carers and that they have done wonders, like I say you know I have got no complaints, but I know from my own experiences that even though the kids are getting on really well and everything else it is still not the same as being at home. (Eddie)

> She is well looked after, she is well cared for but I have still, I still feel that from the way Alice talks, Alice knows it is like a temporary measure, it is not a home home. Even though she knows that she can stay there it is not, she knows it is different from being in a home, a family home. (Amy)

Parents' own attitudes to whether this was a real home would also be likely to influence the child's view of things. Some parents were explicit that the foster home could not be thought about as a real home, but, as this father put it, 'Just a place where my kids are staying at the moment'. He went on to explain his reasons for thinking of the carers and the home itself as no replacement for him as a parent, even though he, too, respects the care his children receive.

> I don't care how nice the foster carers are, you know, at the end of the day as long as my kids are happy and they are treating my kids well then I have got no problems, but I certainly wouldn't hesitate, if there were any problems with any of my kids, to go round somebody's doorway and bang on the door to find out where they are, because they are my children. It is as simple as that. There is no way they are going to be anyone else's children.

The apparently simple statement 'they are my children', backed up by his view that he has rights to fight for them, says much about his view of fatherhood. He has a sense of a relationship that amounts to rights over his children, maybe even ownership, that were not ended or transferred because his children were in care. His identity as a father was a key part of his sense of self and in his own mind he separated out his (conditional) acceptance of the foster carers from his right to a continuing role as a parent. Unlike the previous mother who maintained her role by keeping in touch with the children, he defined his parenthood in terms of his preparedness to fight for them if they were in trouble. His contact with his children was infrequent and he had not seen two of his children for some months because, he said, he preferred to leave them to ask for contact. So the importance of his identity as a father was not necessarily tied to a close and current emotional relationship with his children – and indeed it did not of itself lead to particular parenting actions. But the *idea* of himself as a committed and forceful father was important to him.

Not all parents took a 'simple' view, as this father did, that their identity as a parent was unquestioned. When asked in particular whether their children still saw them as parents, there was often a complex answer, as from this mother.

> Can I take you through it to answer that one? I suppose Carly still thinks I'm her mum, but not a daily mum. Because she knows I am her mum, she knows from the start that I am her mum. I do make the decisions, she knows, at the meetings, because she goes to the meetings. She knows I am there so she knows she has her say and I can have my say, you know we both interact. If they want us to discuss something with her out of the way they tell her to go and play so she don't hear the adults talk so it is more pleasant. But she knows I am there. I think she knows I am her mum. (Joanne)

Joanne took care with her words as she tried to capture a relationship that is not straightforward and there is still some uncertainty as she says 'I suppose…', 'I think…'. In particular, and more concretely, she links her daughter's sense of her as a 'mum' with their joint involvement in meetings. It will not always be the case that birth parents attend meetings, for a range of reasons, but where it happened and was experienced positively, as in this case, the parent could feel part of the team around the child but also respected as a parent in a way that was a signal to the child.

Although this mother saw some limitations in her role (i.e. 'not a daily mum'), she had some degree of confidence in her daughter's sense of her as 'mum'. This was not true for all parents, especially where the child had developed close feelings for the carers and was very much part of the foster family. To try to understand the extent of their perceived role, parents were asked if they thought their children still needed them. This was not an easy question, even for more reflective or accepting parents, because it invited them to imagine how their children might be feeling and to say whether, as parents, they were still needed.

> It is hard. Yes she still needs a mother's influence, but she is getting that from Bridget, her carer. But Bridget is fair, helps me and lets me make some of the decisions and things. I am her mum, but I am her part-time mum really, aren't I? Not through choice, but I do as much as I can. I am a mum to Olivia as much as I physically can be. (Kathy)

This response captures another variation on what a mother can do and be – and another language – a 'part-time mum'. Here there is a more direct sense that in order to evaluate the part she can play as a mother, Kathy needs to take into account some notion of the balance between what she and what the foster 'mother' are offering and the extent to which the child needed both.

This notion of sharing roles in the child's life, sharing the role of 'mother', was evident in a number of interviews. But for some, the response to this difficult question was met with quite high emotion.

And do you think the girls still need you?

> Yes they would be very upset if anything happened, and if I couldn't see them that would be horrible.

What sort of things do you think they need you for?

> They need me there to know that I am still their mum and I will always be there for them and I try and do my best for them and let them know that I care. (Annette)

Where children were said to have strong ties in both families, it was sometimes clear to parents that children were actively trying to *manage* a situation in which both carers and parents were important to them. One focus for this issue might be around what would happen when the children 'leave care', which was seen by parents and (as this quote shows) children as a time when children might be expected to come 'home'.

> Kirsty said to me, 'If I come home, I will still come and spend like a week or something with Dee and Nigel, because she is our mum as well'. So she'd still want to have contact with Dee and Nigel.

What is striking here, and may say something about how open this mother has been able to be or how much Kirsty trusts her not to be angry, is that her daughter felt able to say this to her.

Where parents felt angry and not trusted, then they described their role more negatively – and it is possible to imagine that problems with trust on both sides made it more difficult to work together.

> I just feel like I have been a pushed back mum as you say and some people call it and I think you should have more say, and have things sent to you like their reports… Like when you get a photo of them I don't think it is necessary to cross their badges off, I am not exactly going to go and snatch them, you know I am not a mad person and I get offended. (Annette)

Where parents reflected overall on their loss of identity as parents, it was often in terms of losing the day-to-day tasks that would now be done for the child by the foster carer.

> I could be doing this with my child, getting clothes for her, you know, you don't have that bond, buying shoes, everyday needs, you don't feel… I am still a bit shut out sometimes, but I have to deal with that.
>
> **Right – and how do you deal with it?**
>
> Just don't think about it, I block it out. I don't look at children's clothes.

Such simple examples are poignant reminders that parents are surrounded by images and objects, in magazines, in the shops, on television, that reinforce the fact that they are no longer parents like other parents. Simple tasks, such as buying new clothes, which can create battles but can also provide pleasure for a parent, are undertaken by the foster carers. And for some parents, this amounted to a sense that they had actually ceased to be parents in any significant way.

> I think of them now like they are not our kids.

> **Whose kids do you think they are?**

> The foster carers, because they are the ones who are bringing them up.

Calling the foster carers mum and dad

The question of who *are* the mum and dad and who gets *called* mum and dad led to some very key discussions and some very difficult feelings for parents, even when they valued the child's relationship with the carer. Sharing the role of a mother was not easy for Kathy.

> Olivia calls her Bridget, but very occasionally she will say 'My mum, oh I mean Bridget'. But it hurts; it is something that you would never ever dream of hearing from her lips. It is something I have to accept, but she does know I am 'mummy' if that makes sense. She knows I am mummy and she knows Bridget is Bridget.

Kathy attempts to defend an important distinction – even if her daughter uses the word mummy for both, she knows the difference. This mother defines herself as being the only one recognised as and entitled to the real mummy identity,

Just as this tension about names, identities and roles in the children's lives was there for parents, it was obvious to most that it was also there for the children. Some parents attempted to help their children with their naming problem.

> Yes, yes they know I am their mum, you know they see me as their mum. I am not Lorraine or nothing. They say, 'Mum we love you'. And I send them money and I am 'the best mummy in the world' you know. I get called Mummy. But when I am speaking to them sometimes on the phone and I hear them say to her, 'Mum what are we having for tea?' and then they go 'Oh Dee…', like that and I say, 'No that is alright, you haven't got nothing to worry about. You can call her mum if that makes you happy'.

For Lorraine, there had actually been a point in time when her children asked her if it would be OK to call the foster carers mum and dad.

I even had to let my two girls call their foster carers Mum and Dad. I had to put my feelings aside, bite my tongue, because they wanted to call someone 'Mum' because I weren't there for them. The carers have got a couple of kids of their own and they were hearing them calling 'Mum' and they were saying Dee and Nigel. So Kirsty said, 'Oh we need to ask you something'. I said, 'What is that?' And they sat me down and they said, 'Because you are not there, we can't call you mum. Can we call Dee and Nigel, Mum and Dad?' I had to say yes. Most people say you are mad that you let them call them mum and dad, but I done it for them. The social services said, I have been so good like that letting them do that, you know, for their feelings, for making them feel worth something, for making them feel part of a family instead of a couple of foster kids in care you know. I made them feel, you know, part of their family.

The approval of the social worker for putting the children's needs first is valued by Lorraine. This is an important story and probably quite unusual in the way in which the children ask directly for this permission. But this is not an easy or a simple matter, and Lorraine was unhappy when her willingness to share at least the 'mother' label was not reciprocated. She reported to a social worker how hurt she felt when she was forgotten on Mother's Day – and regrets the foster carer's lack of feeling for another mother.

I didn't get a Mother's Day card from the girls. I said I didn't want a present, but even if it was a piece of paper to say thinking of you on Mother's Day, I love you. And I said the carer should remind them. She is a mother; she should know that Mother's Day matters, I said how would she feel if that was her kids?

There was an acknowledgement among some of the other parents that, however difficult it was for them, their children might want or need to call their foster carers mum and dad.

I think sometimes Carly might call them mum and dad.

If she did, how would that make you feel?

Well it don't worry me because that is natural…, if I was in foster care I most probably would do the same as her, because it is a normal reaction you know. You are living with them twenty four seven, you know, she is bound to call them mum or dad you

> know… Carly used to call me 'old mummy'. You are my old
> mummy, Tessa is my new mummy. (Joanne)

> It is just a name isn't it? Even though Jessica calls them nanny and
> granddad they are not her nanny and granddad, but that is what
> she calls them, so I am quite happy with that. I mean my dad is
> her granddad and she calls him granddad, but she knows the
> difference, she knows that her granddad is her granddad. (Amy)

Again there is a distinction drawn between using names and the 'real'
identity.

Even where there was this recognition that it was understandable
for children to use this family language in the foster family, it could
still reinforce for some parents the long-term loss and a feeling of
rejection by the child; so for these parents, if it did happen they did
not want to know about it. Paula had been told her daughter's foster
placement was to be permanent and was asked how she thought that
would go.

> I don't know. I don't think I want to think about how it could go
> and I don't want it to be happening. You know if Alice is going to
> be calling her mum, and auntie and nanny and all the rest of it
> then fine, but I just don't want to know about it. You know I don't
> want her telling me that she is going to see nanny – no you are
> not because she is working today. Oh no, not that nanny, this
> nanny. Right OK. Well, we will just have to see how it goes. It
> is not nice, you know, and I think that is where I feel the sort of
> rejection from her. Alice is not, you know she is not…she is just
> wanting to fit in, you know, she is fitting in as best as she can. But
> obviously to me it feels like rejection.

Paula had been in foster care herself, but although she understood her
daughter's need to fit in, it did not make it any easier to accept.

> Although it is natural and I did it, you know, when I was in foster
> care, I called her mum, but I can't quite get my head round that
> one, you know, and I think if she started calling her mum I don't
> think I would be able to handle that at all.

Although the stress for Paula and other parents was obvious, the
stress for the children must also be considerable. Children needed to
manage the feelings of both sets of 'parents', without making a slip
and upsetting either. This put particular pressure on contact.

The social worker said 'Oh did you know that she is calling her foster mum 'Mummy' and I went 'What!' I went absolutely mental. But this contact visit that I had, my daughter says, 'But Nanny said this and Nanny said that'. She always calls her 'Nanny' – she doesn't call her Mummy if you know what I mean. (Judy)

In this case the child stuck to the mother's required script at contact, but she obviously needed to take care about she said.

One theme that emerged from the discussion about who was the real parent, and overlapped with the question of who was entitled to the names, was some parents' concern that carers may be encouraging children to treat them as and call them Mum and Dad. This was then contrasted with the (for them) more acceptable carer behaviour when carers were explicit with the children that they were not their parents.

That Ellen (carer) kept saying, 'You can call me Mum', but Alexis is very loyal, isn't she to me, and she wouldn't do it. I think Ellen tried to step in as a new mum and Alexis just wouldn't have it. But I think that Ellen has given up with that now, because Alexis you could pay her a million pounds she wouldn't call anyone else Mum but me. Whereas Esther who has got Kelvin, always says to Kelvin, 'I am not your mum I am just helping your mum out'. (Tina)

Although Tina felt so strongly about her daughter's carer who had tried to 'step in as mum', she did not let that cloud her judgement that this carer was doing a good job.

But as long as that Ellen is good to her, then it don't matter if I don't particularly like her or not... She must be good to Alexis, because Alexis would run away from anywhere even if she had to walk miles and that, and she has never once run away from Ellen's so...

The perceived contrast between carers of different siblings, both in terms of claiming the parent role and claiming the name, was apparent for other parents too.

I mean Jake's carer she has been a carer for forty odd years, she has always let kids know that she is not their mum – she is just looking after them for their mum until their mum is well enough. Dee and Nigel are totally different, they act like they want to be their mum and dad. (Lorraine)

Although carers might be criticised by parents for acting like a mum and dad, for these long-term fostered children there would be an expectation from social workers, independent reviewing officers, fostering panels and courts that in a permanent foster placement, carers would be expected to play more of a parenting role. There may even be expectations that children's relationships with parents would or should become less close in case this was a barrier to permanence.

> Social services have said they are worried about how close me, Holly and Rhys are, which is stupid, because we have to have a bond because we are related. Well, I say if we didn't have a bond it would worry you even more, do you know what I mean? It doesn't make sense. (Gina)

There seemed to be some uncertainty within the system and the families about what exactly the role of parents should or could be. But it also seemed likely that different children with different needs and at different life stages would need different kinds of relationship with carers and with parents. Closeness to a parent may seem obviously valuable, but the relationship may cause some concern if the child is less able to settle in the foster family and is drawn back in the teenage years to a birth family that cannot help and protect them. This is not an argument for encouraging distance between children and parents, but it does suggest a constant need for social workers to help parents to be as supportive as they can be to the child and the care plan – and to help children manage these two families in order to get the best from both, in the longer term.

Managing a threatened identity as a parent

Although, as is apparent from the above and from previous chapters, there was a wide range of feelings and experiences, all parents were acutely aware that their status and identity as parents had been profoundly changed by the fact that their children were in foster care and most parents experienced this as, at times, isolating them and leaving them without a meaningful role. Even where parents did not find that they were criticised or condemned when they told others about their child in foster care, they still had a fear of it, a feeling associated not necessarily with a sense of their own guilt, but with the fact that they had been judged, deprived of their child and thus become outsiders in society.

> It was horrible because when your kids go into care people look at you differently, talk to you differently. (Tina)

This sense of being seen as or even having become a different person was associated with many negative attributions from others. From the child protection interventions and court hearings onwards, parents had heard descriptions of themselves as parents who 'did not care enough' or 'didn't put the child's needs first'. Statements from experts were recalled as having referred to parents as 'being cold', 'lacking empathy', 'making no effort to change'. Worse of all was the language of 'abuse' or 'neglect'. The parents did not recognise such descriptions of themselves and their behaviour. They more often felt themselves as parents to have been, at least to some extent, victims; for example, victims of childhood abuse, drug addiction, violent partners or homelessness. Even where parents recognised their own failings as parents and felt guilty about the lack of proper care of the child, there was always some kind of explanation available that excused their behaviour to some extent and gave them at least a degree of credit for trying to care for their children and, at the very least, for loving them.

Across the diverse positions and emotions that parents described in relation to their children coming into care, there was therefore invariably and for all parents a significant gap between how they thought of themselves and how others – often powerful and expert others, but also people in their extended families and social networks – thought of them. In some cases, there were also gaps between the children's view of their parents as blameworthy and the parents' own view, which were particularly difficult to think about.

But as well as these gaps or inconsistencies between how they were seen and how they saw themselves, parents often struggled with their own contradictory ideas about themselves. Very few parents told the story of their experiences in a way that suggested an entirely consistent view. Thus a father may talk angrily about how he had done his best for the children and there was no reason to remove the children, but then say that it was his heavy drinking that meant the children were not cared for properly. A mother may say that she accepted that her daughter suffered as a result of her drug use and needed to be in foster care, but be angry at the social workers who had 'taken' the children. Of course the nature of these apparently contradictory ideas are also going to be influenced by the messages that parents are getting about what it means to be a parent or a good parent in their culture and community, and their experience of stigma.

Although such contradictory thoughts are common when people are in complex and stigmatised situations and their identity is under threat, the dissonance it creates is in itself a source of stress to the parent. Cognitive dissonance theory (Festinger 1957) proposes that having contradictory cognitions, in particular about one's self-concept or identity, causes psychological stress, raising anxiety and lowering self-esteem. To reduce this stress, a person will strive to modify their attitudes, beliefs or behaviour to experience the world more consistently, in order to protect their self-concept/self-esteem. Aronson (1969) suggests that the level of stress caused by cognitive dissonance was also related to the importance, the salience, of the incompatible cognitions. It seems likely, therefore, that where these contradictory cognitions affect one's self-concept as a parent, which is such a profoundly valued and important identity, the stress of these tensions will be both high and particularly hard to resolve.

For many parents, a central challenge in managing their changed and now threatened identity (Breakwell 1986) was the gap between their sense of themselves as at least having tried to be 'good' parents who loved their children, yet their knowledge that in many cases that they had been 'bad' parents, who had failed their children and that children had suffered harm. For example, parents who accepted that they had harmed children by their drug taking, or by not protecting them from a violent partner, described themselves as having done their best and as having loved their children. Looking back and telling this story it was difficult for them to justify their parenting history in terms of being, nevertheless, a good parent.

Maintaining a 'good parent' narrative

From parents' accounts it seemed that they developed and maintained a number of cognitions/narratives about themselves that attempted to resolve the question of whether they were still properly 'a parent', but also to justify their moral identity as 'a good parent', in contradiction to what had often been said by professionals or may be indicated by the very fact of having children in foster care, and to resolve contradictions in their own judgements of themselves.

Some narratives related to feelings about the process by which the child came into care.

- I am a good parent, because I was not to blame for my child coming into care (e.g. my partner and/or the social worker were to blame).

- I am a good parent, because I always loved my child, even when we had problems.

- I am a good parent compared to some other parents, those who really hurt or do not love their children.

- I am a good parent, but my child was too difficult, too demanding, for even a good parent to manage.

Other narratives about their identity as good parents related to how they had thought or acted since the children had been in foster care.

- I am a good parent, because I accept that foster care is best for my child and support the placement and the carers.

- I am a good parent, because I am taking an active and positive role in parenting my child, even while apart from him.

- I am a good parent, because I have made positive changes to my life, such as giving up drugs, so that my child can be proud of me/may come back to me when older.

- I am a good parent, because I am raising other children successfully.

- I am a good parent because I remain in a constant state of anger and keep fighting to get my child back.

Even with these different identity/self-esteem narratives to counter critical perspectives on their performance as parents, to reassure themselves and to reconcile apparent contradictions into a coherent story, parents needed day-to-day strategies to sustain them. Many parents who needed to maintain that they had not been to blame at all, for example, denied or deliberately pushed away memories of the bad times, before the children were placed into foster care when life was taken over by addiction to drugs or alcohol. If improving their current and future life had become their strategy, some parents forced themselves to think of positive things or work as much as they could, including in some cases working to help other parents, because dwelling on the past was not bearable or helpful and looking to their future identity was essential. Where being angry and continuing the battle with social workers or 'the department' had become the definition of a good parent, parents invested a great deal of time and energy in poring over evidence, making complaints and, in some cases, taking cases back to court.

The message for social work practice from this evidence of diverse strategies for emotion and identity management was that in order to engage with a parent it would be necessary to understand the emotional and cognitive framework in which they were operating. Only this way would it be likely that parents can be helped to maximise their co-operation and contribution to the child's well-being.

Am I still a parent? Managing a threatened identity: key themes and implications for practice

- Parents define themselves as parents in their children's lives in ways that reflect their view both of their biological ties and their actual ability to carry out the role of parent, e.g. they may talk of 'part-time' parenting. Their need is for information and involvement appropriate to their ability to contribute.

- Sometimes parents define their role as parents in terms of being supportive while at other times it is defined in terms of being prepared to fight for their children. Such differences may not reflect greater or lesser commitment to the children but more the personality and identity of the parents.

- Some parents want to maintain a strong identity as parents without necessarily being or wanting to be very involved in their children's lives. This could be a positive or a negative experience for the child, depending on the quality of their foster family life, e.g. a child could feel allowed to make a full commitment to the foster carers or feel abandoned by their parents.

- Parents' perceptions of the parenting role necessarily take into account their view of the role of the foster carers. These roles will be in different kinds of balance in the minds of parents, e.g. they may see both themselves and the carers as active parents or see carers or themselves as playing the role of the 'real' parents.

- For children to name carers 'mum' or 'dad' is seen by most parents as a significant step – though for some it is an unthinkable, unbearable betrayal of their own relationship as a parent, while for others it is seen as a sad but understandable necessity for a child who wants to fit into the foster family or needs to feel they live in a normal family.

- Because their identity as a parent is threatened by the very fact that their children are in foster care, parents develop a range of strategies for managing this threat, such as telling the narrative in a particular way that helps them absolve themselves of some of the responsibility or blame.

- Linked to these strategies, parents need to manage the cognitive dissonance that arises between their sense of themselves as (good) parents and a) the negative perceptions of others and/ or b) their memory of how children had actually suffered in their care.

- It will be helpful for social workers to do a careful assessment of the attitudes, perceptions and strategies of parents in order to be able to work more effectively with them. Understanding how different parents view their role and identity as parents (and what is therefore helpful to them in managing their sadness or anger) may help social workers to offer more targeted support, not only to the parents but also to the foster carers and the children.

9.

Social Workers' Perspectives on Their Work with Parents

It was obviously important in developing messages for social work practice to include the perspectives of social workers on their relationships with parents of children in foster care, here drawn from social worker focus groups. We wanted to understand and give a voice to parents in this research – but we also wanted to hear the other side of what will always be a potentially challenging relationship between parents and case-accountable children's social workers.

Social workers will be involved with parents from the first referral for support or for child protection assessment, through the child coming into care, and then through the years of the child growing up in a foster family. As already discussed, in many local authorities the child's case may move between different teams during this process and social workers may also change for a range of reasons. So from the parent's point of view the 'relationship' will be with a number of social workers. From the social workers' point of view, they are likely to come in at one point in the parent's story and move on after a period of months or years, with only a small number having long-term relationships with parents.

The role of social workers who work with parents of children in long-term foster care will primarily be to monitor and promote the quality and stability of the placement and the child's well-being. The social worker is the key person, on behalf of the local authority and ultimately the state, to ensure that the care plan is fulfilled and the child's needs are met. But although the social worker's primary, and in important ways parental, responsibility is for the child's well-being, this includes facilitating the child's ongoing relationship with the birth family, not only but usually significantly through contact (Schofield and Stevenson 2009).

For all social workers in our focus groups there were clear tensions around the role that they were asked to play, as they balanced their responsibilities to the child, the parents and the foster family. But there are no government or local practice guidelines or procedures regarding this area of work. Different workers and different teams managed the role tensions differently, not only in relation to the amount of time they managed to spend with parents, but in their approach to that relationship. Some social work teams appeared to be too overwhelmed by other demands to give parents the time the social workers themselves acknowledged parents needed, while other social workers, also in busy teams, were somehow finding time to do constructive work with parents, including 'life story work' with parents to help them resolve their feelings about their own childhood and history. When time is a precious resource and in short supply, it is difficult to know what will make this constructive kind of work possible more widely. But certainly social workers who were able to build these more active relationships with parents found them rewarding, as well as valuable when working with the child.

These questions of time and role were bound up to varying degrees with two related issues; attitudes towards parents as entitled and deserving of their time, and empathy for their position. Underlying all these issues when it comes to practice in the context of long-term foster care is the question of how social workers are able to manage their own mixed feelings, including sadness and anger, about both the child's history and situation and the parents' history and situation. These feelings often combine with professional and personal frustration if and when social workers feel unable to 'do the right thing' for the child or the parent or both. They may know, for example, that this is not a perfect foster placement for a child or that resources for contact are not adequate – but nevertheless have to explain and defend the situation to parents. Social workers, too, therefore have difficulties in managing contradictions, between their wish to be effective and helpful practitioners and their awareness of the barriers to achieving good outcomes for children and parents. They will be aware of children whose lives have been transformed for the better by their experiences in foster care, but also of children who may have not been able to settle in a family who could meet their needs.

Social workers need to have a strong sense of the difficulties in the past of parents and children, but also to be able to adjust their view and recognise where there are signs of progress in both. If we look in more detail at how social workers describe aspects of their practice with parents, it is possible to see how these factors (and feelings) link and interact.

Attitudes to parents

Among social workers there was a range of attitudes and expectations regarding parents of children in foster care, which underpinned both the nature of their relationships with parents and specific areas of their practice. Just as parents' varied views of social workers were dependent to some extent on specific characteristics of individual practitioners and to some extent on generalised views of social workers as a group, so social workers' attitudes too could be influenced by specific experiences of certain parents, but also by underlying feelings and beliefs about parents in general.

One dominant theme for most social workers was the powerful sense that, however poor or harmful their care of children had been, most parents could also be thought of as victims of their own past experiences. Social workers were only too well aware from parents' histories that they had often been victims of adversity and abuse, in childhood and adulthood, which provoked feelings of sympathy and concern. But it was also clear to social workers that these kind of experiences in parents' own childhoods sometimes meant that they went on to lack understanding of what was damaging to children in their own parenting.

> What is common to so many of our families is the parents' own experience. Often when you look back and try to understand what it was like for them as children and you see the names, you are starting to see the next generation... They had no role models in effect. So when you actually say, well this isn't good enough, they think, well this is what we know, this is how we were brought up to some extent, and they don't really have the sort of insight that we have perhaps as professionals.

Social workers recognised that where parents lacked understanding or acceptance of the consequences of the poor care they received from their own parents, this could then translate into difficulty for them in taking responsibility for the poor care their own children received.

> I suppose it is quite difficult to accept blame yourself, because it is difficult to blame your own parents isn't it? It is quite difficult to get to the point where you say, well the reason I couldn't give my children the care they needed was because my parents weren't up to it…my parents didn't love me enough.

Though social workers also reported that some parents were quite explicit about the links between their own difficulties and how badly treated they were by their parents.

> So you do get the opposite – some parents will happily admit to how awful it was and sort of be the victim of their childhood, so I think you might get both.

Where parents had been in care themselves, there was an additional sense that 'the system' had failed them. This was experienced by some social workers as a professional and personal responsibility that made them feel additional frustration and sadness, as they were now removing into care the children of parents who had themselves been cared for by the local authority.

> For some parents I feel there is some inevitability about it, because a lot of our parents have experience of the care system themselves or have children who have been removed from them, or other people within the family have at some time had involvement with our department for nigh on twenty or thirty years. I did a number of pre-birth assessments for former care leavers and when I read their files from twenty years ago, we have accountability around that. Our service failed them so much that their lives were really difficult and now they have become a parent and they are struggling as parents and that is probably one of the hardest bits that I have dealt with really.

Managing these difficult feelings of collective responsibility complicates the already difficult balance that social workers are dealing with all the time as they try to ascertain the risk of significant harm to children from remaining in the care of their parents, the implications of separating children from parents when taking children into care –

and the relative benefits that foster care may offer. What is clear here, though, is that that those feelings among social workers include some degree of empathy with and concern for the parents who are facing a significant loss, even while in their professional role social workers recognise the need to intervene to protect the child.

Social work practice when children come into care

Social workers currently with case responsibility for foster children often reflected on whether enough help had been offered to the family early on to parent their children now in care. This question may be around the availability of adult services to help adults who are also parents.

> If adult services (mental health services, substance misuse and learning disability) had actually worked with these parents then there could have been a high possibility of the children staying within their family unit. A lot of the time children's services are picking up the pieces, because adult services don't have the funding from the Government. We are not talking short-term solutions to give up smoking, we are talking long-term psychotherapy that the majority of these families need and deserve so that the children can remain within these families, and the services aren't there, right across the board.

As also described by the parents, social workers reported that although there has usually been work with families for some time, children nevertheless often come into care in a crisis, a process that will itself have an impact on parents as well as children.

> Family support teams have often worked with families for a very long period of time and then a crisis has happened which has led to us thinking right we need to take these children, go to court or take action or seek police intervention or something has happened to trigger that change so my guess is that for parents it might come as a bit of a shock or can be seen as quite heavy handed to do that.

The process of removing children, the day it happens, can be both shocking and distressing to children, parents and social workers – and have a long-term impact on later social work practice with the family.

> Even though we may have talked about it, the whole experience of having the children taken out of their home is, I am sure in their lives, a memory that they return to all the time and then we pick up the flack from that. I think personally when I do that work and take children away from the family, for me it is incredibly difficult and I am the professional. So for them I think it is something we don't always think about when you think about what they have been through.

Given the inevitable stresses for the parents and the social workers, as both also manage the feelings of the children, the value of honesty was important. But these are volatile situations and social workers could feel themselves to be physically at risk.

> I think the main thing or the most important thing I have found about working with birth parents is absolute honesty and transparency. Sometimes that can be incredibly difficult when you are faced with a parent who you might be wary of, where you are not sure about the level of aggression they might have towards you, whether they may be unwell or under the influence of alcohol and drugs, because you are not quite sure about the reaction that you are going to get...

Although it may be tempting for workers not to be honest, even about their anxiety regarding aggression, it can help to be straight with parents.

> I have worked with families where I have actually been quite frightened, one particularly of the father and where the mother had extreme aggression as well. I said, 'You know I will speak to the police if you assault me'. And in fact the father was quite aggressive towards me and she took him out, took him away from me, so she actually stepped in and protected me from him. I think that was part of the relationship that I had with her and the absolute honesty about what was going to happen.

Sometimes the crisis that leads to children coming into care might have been be triggered by the children themselves and the social worker then has the task of safeguarding the children, bringing the agencies together in order to work effectively with the parents.

> A nine year old would walk in with his brothers and sisters and say 'Mum is missing, she is in a crack den, we haven't eaten for four or five days, what do I do?' And then it is engaging the parents

there, the kids are already in care, mum has a drug problem, even if we can find her because she is in various crack dens, and getting her on board, getting her into the court process and all that. It takes a long time and getting all the other services, getting the health visitor, getting all that co-ordinated, that takes time.

As social workers accepted, they are working under such pressure at these times that parents may not get the time they need.

We are operating in crisis as well and often if we need the police involved, the police protection only lasts for three days, you know we need to be preparing statements and gathering the evidence in order to go to court to get an order to maintain the child in our care, to keep them safe. I suppose the priority for us often becomes gathering of the evidence, getting all the paperwork together, which is a massive task in order to do that, and I think the parents' needs get lost in all that, because our priority is the child's needs and maintaining the welfare and the safety of the child.

The social worker also needs both to get and give information to parents who may be still affected by drugs or mental health problems, but will also be in a state of shock. Part of the social work task then was to ascertain the parents' mental state and level of understanding, prior to this urgent need to exchange information.

I suppose we are kind of bombarding them with information as well or asking them lots of questions. The first question is does your child take any medication, what are their routines, are they allergic to anything – those practical things that we need to be able to inform the foster carer about. And then there is the other, why we are removing this child and what you need to do next and sorting out contact and when they might see their child and encouraging them if they are going to court to get legal representation.

It is not surprising that parents remember this period of the children's transition into care as in some ways vivid and painful and in other ways as rather a blur. For social workers, too, managing everyone's heightened emotions at this time combines with the need to make sure that all practical arrangements are made not only at speed but also appropriately and according to procedure. Just as parents may be criticised during child protection and court proceedings if they do not, for example, attend an assessment or keep to contact arrangements, so social workers too may be criticised, not only by parents but also by lawyers, judges, the guardian, foster carers, other professionals and even older children, if there is delay or if they appear to get something wrong. This is the job social workers are trained to do, but there is no denying the pressure they will be under.

The impact of court and the care decision on parents

The role of the court is important in the accounts of parents and social workers, not only because this is a key decision-making point, but also because the power of the court and the nature of the legal proceedings can seem ritualised and unreal.

> It is a strange world, that you all visit and then you disappear and carry on... It's all drama, it is acting.

Social workers were also aware of the clashes of ethnicity, class and culture that families face in the court system.

> Most of our families are from black and ethnic minorities. We go to court and are in front of the bench and we have got very middle class, upper class, majority females that do not speak a language that our clients understand...and our clients are going, what is the point?

Although parents reported that they felt that nobody understood how difficult their experience in court was, for most social workers, the painfulness of the parents' position in the court setting was only too evident. Social workers commented that the adversarial nature of the process left everyone drawing up dossiers of evidence that could be used against each other, which often added to distress and led to an oversimplification of the parents' and the child's complex situation.

> I don't think these proceedings fit very well into the world of the child, because it is adversarial isn't it, the black and white.

But during that assessment and court process, when there is a need to collect evidence to make their case in court, social workers were aware of their instrumental role on behalf of the child into the future, even while they were working with distressed or angry parents.

> You are always trying to gain information, because you are thinking life-story books too. The children will need that information if mum or dad walks out the door – if they can't cope with the final proceedings, they may disappear at that point.

At the point of the decision for a care order at court, social workers were able to see the problems for the parents, problems of loss not only of their children, but of support for themselves. As parents described in previous chapters, there is so much activity and professional contact during an assessment and while a case is going through court and there is also still the hope, however faint, that the court will rule in the parents' favour. But when the final decision is made, both the activity and the hope are at an end, and the social work focus moves on.

> Quite often after the final hearing if the placement for the child is going to be where they live permanently, your relationship changes and you are straight into the plan for the child with the foster carers, and that is where the relationship goes. Whether it has been an antagonistic relationship with the social workers or a good one, parents lose a lot, not just the child. This whole thing that took up their lives has all gone, as well as the child.

Social workers described the parents' experience at the end of the hearing in similar terms to those expressed by parents themselves.

> It is almost as though the spotlight has been on the parents right through care proceedings, with the assessment and everything else. Then the order is made and they are almost abandoned.

> Court often repeats parents' other experiences of abandonment. It is so extreme in their lives that at that final hearing point they have lost their child and they have lost everything.

> After the order is made, all the professionals are saying, 'Oh well that's good, it is all finished'. There's a sense of achievement – but I just think, 'Oh God, this person has just lost her children'.

Although the impact of loss at this point was recognised, social workers were also aware that for some parents, who knew that they were unable to care for their children, the court decision was a relief.

> I think some parents feel quite relieved that a decision has been made. Some parents are kind of aware on some level, particularly

when they have got a number of children, that they are not managing.

Experienced social workers were also able to reflect that, painful as court decisions can be at the time, parents may later see that they were necessary, and workers hold on to this during their work with parents.

> Parents can come back two or three years down the line and say, 'Well you said this and this in court. I didn't accept that at the time, but now I can see why you were worried'. It's about helping parents come to terms with what has happened.

One area of court work involving parents that caused particular concern was where parents made subsequent applications for the discharge of the care order or for contact. This was not a common event, but, as one social worker put it, 'Sometimes it is the same parents taking lots of applications, rather than it being a large number of parents'. The court does have the power to make an order that further applications by parents need to have the leave of the court first (Children Act 1989, section 93), but social workers found that this did not stop the most determined parents and that courts would tend to give leave for an application to be made, even if there was not much evidence that parents had changed.

Whatever the context, applications to court by parents in relation to children in foster placement were said by social workers to be very disruptive for the children. Often children would need to get drawn into the proceedings, with all parties required to take account of the child's wishes and feelings. Children can be torn between contributing to the parents' case, for example by saying they wanted more contact or to go home, or upsetting parents by asking to stay in their foster family. Social workers would need to consult children about the prospect of returning home, even if they had worked hard with the child to help them settle in a permanent foster placement and had reassured them that this was a secure family to grow up in. In addition, children's guardians and solicitors would also be getting involved in consulting the child. These cases could continue for some months, maybe a year, and during that time children and foster families would be uncertain about what would happen next, which could affect not only family life, but also children's school work and their physical and mental health. Although applications for children to return home were rarely successful, one outcome after all these months might be that the court would decide on a 'compromise' whereby the level of contact would be increased, a plan that would not always be justified by the facts or be appropriately child centred.

Whether in the context of the initial court application by the local authority or subsequent applications by parents, the court arena was not the best place to start or develop a constructive and co-operative relationship between social worker and parents. Nevertheless efforts were being made by social workers to build a constructive and supportive relationship even in this difficult situation, and this could make a difference for the subsequent conduct of the case.

> I think it is about the quality of the relationship with a supporting social worker really. You know parents can get stuck on that initial relationship for a very long time if it hasn't been OK and if it has been OK I think one of the structural problems we build in is the loss of that relationship…there can be a loss of a helping professional who might have done a difficult thing, but they are building something at a time of crisis, and parents lose that, and then they have to regain that with another social worker. But when you see kind of calm outcomes from the final hearing you can see the quality of the social work is there and when you see messy outcomes you will often see multiple social workers.

Relationships with parents

The importance of good quality and continuity in practice and the range of different kinds of relationships between social workers and parents that developed were described by parents in previous chapters. Here they are described from the point of view of the social workers.

The degree to which working with parents felt like a partnership, as proposed in the Children Act 1989, was quite varied, and seemed to reflect some differences in agency resources and workers' attitudes as well as differences in parents' capacity to work co-operatively. Some social workers would actively involve parents in most cases, in particular promoting openness between the parent and the foster carers.

> If the parent presented no particular risk to the placement, I would always take the parent to placement with me, sort out contact

arrangements, and get them to talk directly with the foster carer about the child.

Where parents were accepting that children needed to be in care, it was possible for social workers to more actively involve parents in the arrangements for their children's foster placement – even the decision about different sibling arrangements.

> I did work on a case where there was five children and the two oldest ones were in our care and three younger ones were then on the Child Protection Register and it was planned that the younger children would come into our care. Court proceedings were initiated and the mother was involved in talking to the foster carer about the foster placements, which children she thought should be placed together, and a decision was made for the two youngest to be placed together and the other one separately. She visited the placements with the children before they came into our care and she developed a good relationship with the foster carers and was involved a lot in that. I think that, in fact, she probably still has a good relationship with the department.

Other social workers and managers had had difficult experiences that had made them more pessimistic about the involvement of parents. One manager suggested that the vast majority of parents were likely to be negative towards the placement and that establishing a good working relationship was only possible for a small number. It was argued that this was too much to expect when it had been social workers who had removed the children in the first place.

Although social workers differed, even within the same local authority, as to the proportion of parents who they believed would be able to work constructively with social workers, all accepted that there was a wide range of parents and that it was very important for social workers to distinguish between the most positive or flexible and the most negative or fixed in terms of their capacity to accept the child living in foster care. This account fits well with the evidence from the parents in this study.

> I think the parents who can learn to live with their children being in foster care are the parents who can enter into a dialogue, and some parents just can't, they are always going to be confrontational; 'It wasn't me, you didn't give me a chance. If you had let me have a mother and baby unit...' And they never seem

> to move out of that. And there are other parents who can move forward and can appreciate, 'I am really pleased he is doing well at school'

Although parents were seen as varied in their ability to move on and to work with social workers, as in the court setting, this was seen as affected by the quality of the social work practice.

> But it is how you enable a parent to have that dialogue when you are seen as a controlling, authoritarian social worker. Again that is a real skill that social workers need, to protect the children, but allow them to have a good enough relationship and a safe one with the parents, so the parents can be proud of their children who are not their children any more.

Not all parents were able to overcome their sense of anger and for those (a minority) who built their identity on their need to do battle with social workers, even good social work practice may only make a modest difference. Here the focus may have to be on protecting the child.

One of the areas that parents have raised consistently was the need for *information* from social workers about the children in order to maintain a sense of connection and a role as parent. Social workers found that responding to the specific needs of each parent to enable them to stay engaged in a dialogue about the children often meant being active in how information was communicated. Sometimes helping a parent to be involved and to feel they are still a parent took extra efforts as a result of the parent's own vulnerabilities. One social worker talked of having to use visual methods, in this case photographs, to help a parent keep track of her memories of contact and to build a sense of a continuous relationship with her children over time.

> One of the mums, her long-term memory isn't there because of the alcohol and drug abuse. So we have taken photos for each of the contacts going back two or three years and because she has got the photos and we talk about each contact she remembers it, because visually she can see it and think about it. If you try and get her in date order of even two or three weeks ago she would struggle with that, but because we date them she is then able to say, 'Well I have got a picture, we met at that place, we did that you know'. That worked really well.

This kind of sensitive practice with a parent takes time, but in transforming the parent's experience would almost certainly enrich the experience of the child, who would also have these photos of each contact to help share memories with her mother.

Although social workers accepted the need for certain kinds of information to go to parents regularly, they did feel there was a lack of official guidance about what was appropriate – and expressed concerns that sometimes parents were making demands for information that were understandable but unrealistic.

> In terms of us having a duty to inform parents it would be around health, education and contact, because they are discussed in the review. However, some parents want to know what they had for Christmas dinner, you know, and they expect a written report about what that child had and they want a list of all their Christmas presents, they want to know about their haircut, so there are different levels of information.

Decision making in long-term placements

As this list of the kind of information parents may want suggests, such decisions as those concerning children's diets and haircuts continue to preoccupy some parents after the point at which they are able to make or often be involved in making those decisions. It is part of the social worker's negotiation of the role of the parents to consider both the official decision-making processes and their own role as mediators between parents and foster carers. Social workers disagreed about where the power to make most decisions lay – parents, foster carers or social workers.

One social worker saw their own role as central.

> You are the broker in the middle, because you know that the foster carer can't make a lot of decisions and the parent isn't allowed or supposed to.

But others saw foster carers as powerful in the situation. As these questions of information giving and decision making suggest, social work with the parents will nearly always be in the context of managing the relative contribution of foster carers and parents to the life of the child. Although social workers were viewed as ultimate decision makers in the context of the care order, there was a consensus that foster carers would have a greater part to play in day to day decision making than parents and that this would affect how parents experienced their own role. They also recognised that over time, in a long-term placement, the balance in the network of relationships can change and carers would and should be allowed more scope to make everyday decisions;

> What might have happened at the start of the placement and what might happen two or three years down the line I think are different. If the child is remaining in long-term foster care and they are going to live in that foster family, then that family in the longer term are going to take more of those decisions around getting the haircut, the change of school and the transition phase between primary and secondary. The day to day parent is going to be the one who takes those decisions, you know, how much pocket money is given, what clothes are bought and those sorts of things.

This question of who is the 'day to day parent' is at the heart of how permanence in foster care is experienced by all parties. Social workers, who are responsible for implementing the care plan, wanted to be clear about how this could be managed in each case and what is desirable and possible.

> There can be and should be some negotiation on an individual basis about what role parents take, because there is no reason why the birth parent can't be involved in some of those day to day things. I think it is entirely about the relationship which has developed between the foster carer and the birth parents.

What was suggested by social workers to be missing in the current practice situation was a 'forum', a meeting of the carer, the parent and the social worker, where some of these issues about different parental roles in long-term cases, and in particular the parenting tasks of foster carers and parents, could be discussed.

> In an ideal world with long-term cases you would have a forum where people could talk about how you are the mum here and how I am the mum there and how this person is the corporate mum and actually have that conversation with people. But you know we don't have the time for that and we don't have the facilitators. But that to me is what would make the difference.

This was seen as a very different kind of meeting to the LAC review – to which parents were often not invited in some areas, a decision generally taken by the Independent Reviewing Officer. This reflected conclusions that were discussed in earlier chapters that there needed to be different types of meeting and discussion. It often seemed from parents' accounts, from these social workers and from other research (Schofield and Ward *et al.* 2008), that the LAC review may too often be used as a place to discuss things that might be better dealt with in less formal meetings between social workers and parents or between parents and foster carers. Key to this practice issue was the need to find time and strategies to promote more constructive relationships between the various 'parents' in the life of the chid.

> These relationships – the whole point of our job is about relationships, and often we miss that out.

The importance of the fostering social workers

The social workers consulted for this research were those with primary responsibility for working with parents, the children's social workers. But what emerged from these discussions was that the quality of relationships between foster carers and parents was likely to be determined to a large degree by the approach taken by the recruitment and supervising social workers from the fostering teams. Children's social workers felt that fostering social workers may be more likely to discourage a relationship between the carers and the parents.

> The family placement teams, recruitment teams are not really pushing foster carers to be open to the idea of getting in touch with birth parents, having relationships with birth parents.

Supervising social workers will have different priorities, for example avoiding pressure on carers and placements from 'difficult' parents, and may encourage carers to avoid risk and to feel that it may not be necessary or appropriate or safe to communicate directly with parents. As social workers commented, basic training for carers provides information on the impact of abuse and neglect, and inevitably often emphasises how children have been damaged by their birth families, including the risk of harm to the infant's brain development from neglect and abuse. So it is perhaps not so surprising that many foster carers become very protective of children, but rather wary of parents. If there is then no forum for carers and parents to meet, as suggested above, carers may hold onto these ideas about parents in general or this child's parents in particular, without getting the opportunity to achieve more balance and see the range of parents. This can have an impact not only on their potential for carers to have a relationship with the parents, but also on the extent to which carers can help the child come to terms with the past, present and future relationships with their parents.

It was also suggested that there will be carers who do take against certain parents, a problem that needed to be recognised and managed between the social workers.

> I think we still have foster carers who openly show their dislike for parents and you would just hope that that never ever happens, but actually it is far more common than you think it is. Parents are very aware that this foster carer doesn't like them.

The parents' accounts certainly provided many examples of foster carers who were very accepting of parents and worked with them with warmth and consideration, in a relationship supported by social workers. But not all relationships are like this and most need to be managed jointly by both the child's and the carer's social workers, as the child will be experiencing either the benefits of co-operation among parents, carers and social workers or the stress of unresolved tensions.

Contact

Much of the focus of social work activity with parents was said to be around contact, with the need to maintain children's family ties through contact seen in some areas as having had an increasingly high profile in recent years. In this area too, relationships, both between social workers and parents and between foster carers and parents, needed to be carefully managed with the child in mind.

Although promoting contact for looked after children, in so far as it is in their best interests, is a generally accepted principle, the decisions about the frequency and supervision of contact would be made based on a range of factors. These would include how accepting and supportive the parents were of the placement and, to some extent, the degree to which they demonstrated that they could work co-operatively with the social workers and carers, as this increased the level of trust.

> If parents don't behave in a way that is seen as being responsible and not undermining of the care plan or the placement, then the likelihood is they may well have contact reduced or they may have contact structured in a way that is more or less supervised, or there is more support than they want.

One factor in contact decision making was said to be maintaining the focus on the needs of the child when decisions about contact were made. It was suggested that this focus might appear to be threatened by social workers from adult services who were concerned for the parents.

> Sometimes I find adult services are so focussed on the parents that they lose what we are trying to do with the child. So adult services might say, oh it is really important for this parent to have contact, because I don't know what is going to happen to them if they don't see their child or they might start misusing drugs if you don't let them see the child. Well actually contact is about the children not the parents.

Decision making about supervision of contact as children grew older and parents perhaps changed was never easy. Although it seemed appropriate to reduce supervision for older children, there were still often concerns even with teenage children about the impact of contact. One social worker reported how a temporary social worker had not read the files fully and had agreed to unsupervised contact that led to a long-term fostered teenage girl abandoning a promising academic career and dropping out of school.

But it was often hard for social workers generally to make these decisions about contact when they did not know the parents well. One social worker explained that as there was an annual cycle of contact planned in advance, she would discuss this with the parents, but would not then expect to have any meetings with the parents during the year. This fitted into a general picture of social workers not expecting or having time to prioritise work with parents, but it also followed from what is now common practice for contact to be supervised by a specialist supervisor rather than the child's social worker.

> I think there is a gap in our service whereby when a child becomes looked after we tend to put the parents on a back burner, i.e. we are the allocated worker for the child and we focus on the child and I think that is an issue with the contact supervisor service, in that no one does actually work with the parents.

One social worker commented that if she had time to make one phone call after contact it would probably be to the contact centre or the carers to make sure the child was well and safe. It might be harder to find the time, or maybe the emotional energy, to make what would often be a very difficult call to the parent to see how they were feeling about the contact. In this context, it would be important for contact supervisors to be as far as possible linked to specific families so that there is continuity for the children and the parents, but also so that there could be regular feedback to the case-responsible social worker and the foster carer. Without professionals knowing both the birth and the foster family and mediating between them, it may be the child who alone carries the burden of managing this potentially complex relationship.

A theme that has emerged throughout this book has been that sibling groups raise special issues for parents, but also for social workers who need to place and manage the placements of all the siblings as well as help parents maintain an appropriate role with children of different ages in sometimes different placements. Contact often defines these differences, not only in types of placements, but in the attitudes of different carers to contact, all of which social workers have to manage.

> The foster carer has a very pivotal role in terms of support and not undermining that contact. I have worked with foster carers, where there have been large sibling groups with children placed in different foster placements. Some of the children will get contact and some of them won't, and that is mainly I think about the different foster carers.

Although establishing contact was seen as generally positive, social workers could see how the different placements and contact arrangements for sibling groups could put overwhelming pressure on individual children who, as we have also seen from parents' accounts, may start to play a highly significant role in the minds and lives of their parents.

> The mother has got four who have gone to adoption, so she has said goodbye to them, she has contact with the two that are left, but one, the oldest one has now been placed in a permanent placement, and she has said, 'I can't see you anymore, I can't deal with this, I am angry with you.' So there is intense pressure on the one that is left. And the son that she has got contact with was the child that she didn't want, the child that she didn't bond with. But now, because he is the only link and the only possible child that she is going to see, he is the best thing in the world, he is everything and it is almost too intense for him when she sees him, 'I love you', 'I love you too'. I mean like that book 'I love you to the moon and back', 'No I love you further than that' and he is overwhelmed, and that so often is the case with some parents.

This analysis by the social worker supports some of the conclusions it was possible to draw from the parents' descriptions. The need of the parent for at least one child to give them a focus for all their sense of loss and need to maintain a parenting role can place the child in an impossible situation. Where, as in this case but not unusually, the child has previously been rejected by the mother and longed for her attention, it is even harder to achieve some kind of balance. But undoubtedly this child would need not only someone to work closely with him and to help him cope with this relationship, but also someone to work with the mother to find ways to reduce the pressure on the child.

One difficulty for many social workers and carers when trying to manage an appropriate level of contact, in terms of frequency and emotional demands, was that for older children the mobile phone had made this kind of management of contact almost impossible. For parents, the mobile phone was the mainstay of their freedom to have a relationship of their own choosing with the child. But for social workers and carers it could be a threat to all their work to establish and stabilise the child in the foster family, in school and in prosocial peer groups.

> Since the advent of mobile phones, the myth that we actually control levels of contact has gone by the by. In the last five years, with mobile phones, parents have the ideal opportunity to undermine absolutely everything. Even when we supervise

contact there are still kids, young people who will go to the ends of the earth to get a parent's mobile number and then there are parents who will text, seven, eight, nine, ten times a day to their child and it is a huge issue because parents can vent whatever they want to.

Although there are situations where parents and children accept some limitations to the number of phone calls, and in fact are quite glad to have some guidance on this, there will be some parents and children for whom control is not possible. This places additional burdens on the child, but also responsibilities on the social worker and the foster carer to try to work with the child and the parent to gain their co-operation in keeping both the frequency and the emotional demands to a level compatible with the child's welfare.

Taking a life-span perspective: life story work with children and parents

One of the areas of work with the child that benefits from work that is done with the parents (as well as other family members) will be life story work. As mentioned above, from the earliest involvement with a family and through court proceedings, social workers were aware of the need to gather a full family history with the child's future needs in mind. Some information needs to be collected to ensure that the child has a complete and coherent story of their lives to date, but other information will have specific significance for the child's future. Not all children in long-term foster care will have the same kind of rigorous check of medical records that happens in adoption, yet genetic inheritance is an important issue for these children too. One social worker described a case in which through talking to the birth mother at length it transpired that there was a family history of breast cancer, the kind of history that would be important for the foster family as well as the social worker to know about and to be able to share with the child in later years.

What emerged more surprisingly, but convincingly, from the social workers' accounts of their work were the benefits of doing the equivalent of life story work with parents. It is accepted that parents have complicated histories in childhood and adulthood and these include not only adversities such as poverty and neglect, but growing up in complex families in which sibling groups may have different fathers and the accuracy of their family tree may not be known for certain. In some cases this work may be done as part of the work to help a parent move on from the loss of the child. Here the collecting of information by a social worker enabled two albums to be made, one for the child and one for her mother.

> The mother did meet the foster carer before the baby was born so it was very well planned, we knew what was happening. So for her she had a sort of life story book. We even found some postcards that were of Ireland, because her family come from Ireland originally, and somehow I got one that had a map of Ireland and it had the village where mum, where the grandmother was born so we had things like that in there and for her that was very therapeutic. She didn't get the baby back, but you know she is out there and she has got this album and anything we have got we add to it. She calls in to see if I am around, if I am not she will leave a message to say she has been in.

Although this example related to the parent of a child placed for adoption, there are very useful lessons for working with parents in foster care. It is clear that the parent is seen as somebody who has needs of their own and that acknowledging that established a relationship with the social worker that the mother still felt able to draw on.

In a more complex case, a father who had been adopted, but experienced maltreatment and then came into care, was concerned about what would happen to his baby in the care system or if adopted. The social worker took the trouble to go to see his adoption file in another authority and found evidence that confirmed his account of his difficult experiences.

> I managed to get his adoption certificate for him because he had lost it along the way or never had it, I don't know, and his original birth certificate. I managed to trace, with the help of a colleague, an ex social worker to him, who we approached and asked if she would write something about her memories of him and his family and the things that happened you know to get him where he was.

From this account it seems that the work with the parent may need to go well beyond collecting evidence for court or even for the child's life story book. This work was actively aimed at helping the father to resolve some of his difficult feelings from the past, seeing him as someone with needs of his own and someone entitled to help in his own right. But he was also a young man who may well go on to have further children and if his experiences during the loss of this child can help him achieve a coherent narrative about the past and his feelings about it and prepare to be a successful father then this must be time very well spent.

In this team, social workers talked of the great value of being available to parents – but also of the value of being part of a staff group in an office where parents could pop in and know that the receptionist would know them and greet them respectfully.

> Parents will come in and they will sit there and say right can you just see if Susie (social worker) is in today? No she is not; let's have a look where she is. And they show them the screen, so they can see whether she is in or out, no she is not going to be around until three, well would you like to leave her a message? … They are happier because they actually feel that you have done something, that they have been listened to.

This acceptance of continuing availability, where possible, for parents of children in care was recognition of the need for a life-span perspective in practice, in which the lives of children and parents would continue to evolve alongside, but meshed with each other in these long-term placements.

Conclusion: what do social workers think parents need from them?

Social workers' views of what parents needed from them were almost entirely in agreement with what parents themselves said they needed. *Continuity* was seen by parents and practitioners as important but hard to achieve, whether for structural reasons (e.g. cases moving between teams) or simply because social workers moved on or were promoted. The corollary of continuity was the possibility and benefits of a relationship, and this it was said needed to be a relationship based on *honesty, openness* and *trust* – on both sides. As one social worker and her team leader emphasised, this was key to how they worked with parents.

Parents all say the same thing to us, 'You are honest with us, you tell us the truth…' and that is the contract we work from. Sometimes you are unpopular and we have had big fall outs from it, but honesty is such a big thing and that is where the trust comes from.

Social workers' perspectives on their work with parents: key themes and messages for practice

• For social workers, there are tensions as they balance their responsibilities for the child, the foster placement and the parents. These tensions are in part to do with time and resources, but can also be linked to ambiguities in their helping role when they have also been either directly responsible or are representatives of the organisation responsible for removing the children or keeping them in foster care.

• Social workers recognised the impact of court and the care decision on parents and felt a great deal of empathy and concern for parents who experienced both loss and a sense of abandonment.

• There were wide variations between agencies, teams and individuals in how they practise, viewed and managed relationships with parents. This is an area of practice in which local cultures and attitudes can be influenced by particular managers and practitioners, who may actively work for more openness and collaboration or may be more pessimistic and give this work lower priority.

• The role of family placement social workers in recruiting and supervising/supporting carers is likely to have a significant impact on the relationships with parents that develop and the role that parents are able to play. Any policy to promote effective work with parents would need to include this group of practitioners.

• Contact can take up a massive amount of social work time, especially where there are siblings, but often the task of helping parents to anticipate and plan for contact (or recover and resolve feelings afterwards) is not a priority. As we have learned from parents, contact may give great pleasure, but can for some be experienced as an ordeal. Children almost certainly feel the same. Social workers were well aware that this aspect of their work with parents needed to be addressed if at all possible.

• Life story work with children drew on the quality of work with parents, but life story work of a kind with parents may also have benefits for parents and children in the longer term. Most significant is the life-span perspective implied here not only within a long placement but in the intergenerational transmission of parenting problems and separation into care.

• Continuity, openness, honesty and trust all mattered to parents – and this was recognised by social workers as key to good social work practice, although structural factors and resources need to support this kind of work.

10.

Conclusion: Developing Social Work Practice

This book has set out to inform social work practice by providing a detailed account of what parents of children growing up in foster care say about their thoughts, feelings and changing lives. The implications for social work practice at each stage have been identified and then put in the context of social workers' views of their roles and relationships with parents.

Here we will focus on four ways of thinking about the challenges and opportunities of remaining child focussed while developing a model of social work practice with parents:

- understanding and supporting the parent's journey through placement

- working with relationships in fostering triangles

- working with relationships in wider networks round the child

- managing permanence with parents in mind.

The aim in this final chapter is to think about how the messages of this research can inform not only work with parents, but also work with foster children, foster carers and the networks of families and professionals who surround them.

Understanding and supporting the parent's journey through placement

We are familiar with thinking about the *child's* journey through placement (Fahlberg 2001), but this study has highlighted the significance of understanding the *parent's* journey also. Just as foster children change developmentally in how they manage their history and their current situation in a foster family over time, and may grow closer to or away from their foster carers or parents, so parents also reach different life stages and may grow closer to or away from their children. Parents' view of what brought the children into care and how the children are developing in care may change if their life situation changes, if they become more resolved or reflective as they get older – or if aspects of the children's situation changes. Linked to this change process in relation to parents' attitudes to the *child's* situation is the possibility that parents may develop more or less confidence in the *foster carers* and the foster placement over time, and more or less trust in the *social work* support they receive. Key here is the picture of *diversity* among parents and in how they face and manage this journey.

Social workers with responsibilities for children, parents and foster carers, therefore, need to be aware of the evolving nature of parents' experience. Over the course of a placement, social workers are supporting and monitoring the well-being of children, but also supporting and monitoring the well-being of parents and foster carers. This research supports the idea that each stage requires practice that retains a child focus, but also pays attention to the changing needs of parents.

When children first come into care

While children are being cared for at home, parents who have brought damaging experiences from their own childhood and adult relationships into their parenting will need both intensive and ongoing support. But there will always be families where the judgement is made by the parents that they cannot cope any longer or by social workers and other professionals that the care of children is not good enough and that, in spite of support, children have experienced or are at risk of significant harm necessitating a permanent placement outside of the family. Although some parents continue throughout placements to argue that their children should not have been removed from their care, others feel (at the time or over time) that the decision was right for the children. Some parents report that there were occasions where children were returned to them from short-term care, when perhaps family situations had not improved enough and children were again at risk.

Others suggest that children had suffered for too long, perhaps from a violent partner, and should have been removed earlier. So although it may seem inevitable that all parents oppose intervention and see it as unjust, this is not always the case, at the time or subsequently, even though fighting for their child may be the most common and understandable reaction.

But whatever the range of feelings and attitudes of parents at the time when children come into care, they need clear messages from social workers about the impact on the children of harmful care, in order for them to understand as far as possible the basis for the decision. Social workers in this study described their efforts to achieve this type of communication, though for parents who are struggling with their own difficulties, the official explanation of why it is happening, and what may happen next, is hard to take in. For those parents who are holding on to the hope that foster care is temporary and that children will be returned, it may be impossible for some time to let themselves hear an explanation from the social worker that includes the possibility that the children will be living in foster care throughout their childhood.

Social workers are managing finely balanced assessments and decisions when children first come into care. They are not just part of a network of information and professional opinion, they are at the centre of it. Although the 'decision' that a child is not adequately safe and thriving at home in the care of their parents is the responsibility of the local authority and the court, for the social worker there is a highly personal as well as professional sense of individual responsibility to get the decision right (Hollis and Howe 1987). Very often inquiry reports and serious case reviews where children have died or been injured have suggested that social workers sometimes got too caught up with the problems and needs of the parents and lost the focus on the child (Reder, Duncan and Gray 1993). But the argument must be that *both* child and parent need to be in focus in order for the right decision and intervention to be made and the appropriate support to be offered to the children and the parents – an area of work that requires supportive and reflective supervision from a team manager.

During and after court
By the time children become the subject of care proceedings, parents in almost all cases have experienced great difficulties in their lives,

their relationships and in caring for their children. Their identity and role as parents prior to court will often have developed in the context of anxiety, adversity and fear of losing their children. This can leave many parents overwhelmed by grief and/or anger and, because of the power and ritual of the court, they often feel powerless. Feeling powerless with so much at stake can leave parents stuck in anger or despair. There will also be some parents who are difficult to engage who have gradually cut themselves off from their parenting role and responsibility, and reject or blame individual children for the family's difficulties. Parents demonstrating a range of anger and distress during the court process, therefore, need to be differentiated and understood in terms of important variations in their attributions of blame and responsibility, their parenting capacity and their commitment to each child.

The court will rightly be attempting to weigh the evidence and make their decision within an acceptable timescale for the child's development, health and well-being. But whatever their parenting history and the impact on the child, all parents will need appropriate help and support from social workers during proceedings and, as this research has highlighted, in the period immediately after court. When most professional contacts with parents during proceedings include some element of assessment and 'evidence' gathering, it may seem almost impossible to make the experience any more bearable for parents. Yet the way in which parents experience court can be helped by professional practice that is reliable, honest and offers empathy and concern. Social workers in this study who took responsibility for children's cases after court, commented on how work with parents at that stage can depend on how well the social work task in court was conducted. Of course, parents' experience of court will not depend only on social work practice. The approach taken to parents by the children's guardian, lawyers and judges will also be making a difference. Parents talked of their distress when they felt ignored or unfairly criticised by legal practitioners, but also of the comfort they took from solicitors who supported them and judges who were able to balance their judgements with acknowledgement of the stresses that parents had been under.

Care planning for permanence

Where children are growing up in foster care, they are likely to be the subject of a (more or less explicit) plan for permanence, an expectation that they will remain in foster care, and in a particular foster family, through to leaving care, if not into adulthood.

The way in which parents in this study experienced the transition from being the parent of a child in temporary foster care to the parent of a child in a longer-term, permanent placement suggested that some may not have been aware of the significance of the plan. Rather than seeing this as a social work plan in operation they often criticised the permanent carers for not allowing as much contact or as being less welcoming to them as parents than the short-term carers they met during proceedings. However, most parents by the time of interview were aware that there was a plan for the children to remain in foster care throughout childhood. Although parents might talk of fighting to get the children back, there was no sense that they thought that social workers or courts were still considering this possibility.

As important, perhaps, was the question of the meaning of permanence in terms of the care plan expectation of changes in parenting roles and responsibilities. The question of permanence and its impact on parents is discussed further below, but from the care planning point of view, the shift to a new role for the parents in the context of a new role for carers needs to be handled carefully but openly. As one study of care planning for permanence in foster care has shown (Schofield and Ward *et al.* 2008), local authority procedures rarely explicitly include parents as part of the process of consultation in planning for permanence, nor are parents clearly involved in the renegotiation of roles that may follow, especially if they are not invited to be present at Looked After Children reviews or are not fully involved in the review process.

During long-term placements

The experience of being the parent of a child or a sibling group of children who will live as part of a foster family throughout childhood leads to a number of powerful feelings that have been illustrated and discussed throughout this book. Managing, and for some parents perhaps resolving, feelings of loss, regret, anger, grief, guilt and blame is not easy when there are frequent reminders both of the absence of their children and the stigma that attaches to parents of children in care.

Social workers who work alongside parents during these years will often be aware of the painfulness of the parents' position. At times this will help them to be more active and attentive to the parents' needs. But when social workers find the parents' situation too painful to think about, they may find themselves struggling to tune in to the needs of the parent and therefore rather keep their distance. In contrast, social workers (and other professionals) may become so preoccupied with the parents' difficult situation that they find it difficult to be child focussed. This balance and the feelings associated with it need some help to resolve. Parents will often be challenging to social workers, whose visits or phone calls may stir up past and present feelings of loss and resentment. But this may also be the only opportunity the parent has to talk about those feelings and to work towards some sort of resolution.

Contact, where it is well organised and supported, may provide both a relationship with the children and some solace, albeit also reminding parents of their loss of a full parental role. But although some parents approach contact with the children's needs very much in mind and use contact in a positive way that promotes the child's well-being, other parents will not be able to focus on the child rather than their own needs. Social workers therefore need simultaneously to monitor the quality of the contact for the child and also for the parent with a view to promoting security for the child and preventing risk of further harm (Beek and Schofield 2004b; Cleaver 2000; Schofield and Stevenson 2009; Sinclair 2005). But the overall message must be that making the contact experience as enjoyable and rewarding as it can be for parents is likely in very significant ways to make contact more enjoyable and rewarding for the child.

Making the parents' experience of being a parent as constructive as possible during long periods of separation from their children requires awareness of the significance of communication, information and appropriate involvement. Again, differentiating the capacity and needs of such a wide range of parents means important professional judgements need to be made about the role that each parent can usefully play and how each parent can best be helped.

Adolescence and leaving care

Parents will continue to be important figures as children develop through childhood and adolescence, but they may often play even more crucial roles during the transition to adulthood, as young people develop their identity and plan for their adult life. Parents may support the placement and ensure that gains made in foster care are sustained, or they may create threats to the stability of placements and the likelihood of young people's smooth transition to prosocial and secure adult lives. At each life stage for the child, whether it is moving up to secondary school or facing further education and career choices, or coping in adolescence with the consequences of offending behaviour or early pregnancy, the parents are likely to be part of a network of adults around the child whose views will be sought, but also whose opinions will almost certainly continue to matter to the child.

Although much of the focus on working with parents of children in foster care is about coming into care, court and the early years of care planning and achieving placement stability, the later years when children are in adolescence and then the transition to adulthood are also critical to outcomes (Stein and Munro 2008). In both the child's and the parents' journey through placement, the destination in terms of the quality of the young person's functioning, relationships and stability in adult life will depend on ensuring that the transition to adulthood is handled with very great care, which includes taking account of the role of the birth family as well as the foster family in their lives.

Working with relationships in fostering triangles

What we can see in the simple diagram below of immediate relationships around the child is that there are a number of dyadic relationships (foster carer/child, parent/social worker), but also a number of relationship triangles. The external triangle is that of the three 'parents' in the life of the child – carer, parent and social worker – who have varied roles and responsibilities in relation to the child as well as varied relationships with each other. The internal triangles all include the child and suggest ways in which, for example, two of the

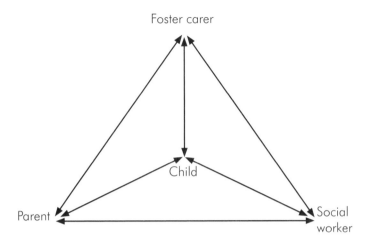

parents (parent/foster carer) might be negotiating within a parent/ foster carer/child set of relationships, which at times replicates the co-operative or conflictual potential of any family and yet is specific and different.

Close alliances in one dyadic relationship, say between carer and child, may exclude the third person, perhaps the parent or the social worker. Similarly, close alliances between parent and child may exclude the carer. On the other hand, closeness need not mean exclusivity, and it was often (but not always) the case that where children had a particularly warm and open relationship with a carer, this extended to include warm and constructive relationships with the birth parents and the social workers.

Each member of these relationship triangles has a part to play in promoting or putting at risk other relationships. This has implications for all aspects of social work practice. Thus the quality of the relationship between the *child* and the *parent* will to a large extent depend on the *carer's* ability to help the child manage this relationship, perhaps by understanding the family history in a balanced way or helping the child to talk though their mixed feelings about contact. But it will also depend on the carer giving the parent the message that, for example, they are not judging them and can understand their feelings about seeing their children. Although the social worker is not part of this triangle, an awareness of the need to make this triangle work, so that no one party feels ignored or unheard, means that they have to monitor how it is operating and how people are feeling, and offer support as necessary. It may be necessary to offer parents direct support, but it may equally be important to assist the parent by talking to the carer and dispelling any negative myths about the parents that may have arisen. On the other hand, there may be cases where the foster carer becomes so close to a parent that the child starts to feel excluded or blamed, and here too the social worker needs to intervene to ensure the carer remains child focussed.

Communication within dyadic relationships and triangles is very significant and at times dyads and triangles need to get together. Parents and carers, and parents, carers and social workers, should meet together at times to allow shared and different parenting issues, thoughts and feelings to be aired and negotiated. Pleasures and/or concerns about the child's progress and ideas for the future can both be shared. The current tendency to proceduralise communication has led to an insistence on all gatherings being formal, having an agenda, being minuted, having an independent chair and ensuring the child is present. This may be important as a corporate reviewing process, but it should not be the only context in which people meet, talk, get to know each other and try to manage boundaries in a way that helps the child to feel that parents are getting on. As this research has shown, not all relationships, especially between parents and carers, can become fully relaxed and co-operative – as is to be expected. But where even some degree of collaboration is achieved, it can enhance the whole network of relationships – and the child's experience.

The balance of power to make decisions as well as the degrees of closeness in these dyads and triangles will vary between cases, depending on such factors as the child's needs and the expectations of the relative roles of carers and parents. These also will vary over time as children's needs change and parents and carers are expected to respond appropriately, both to the child and in the context of the permanence plan. It is this longer-term perspective, in the context of an inevitable sharing of certain aspects of parenting, that leads to the final discussion of the book – the nature of permanence in foster care and the implications for parents and the role of social workers. But first it is important to look briefly at wider networks.

Working with relationships in wider networks round the child

Although the focus of practice will often be social work relationships with the child, the carers and the parents, there are wider family and professional networks around the child that need attention. It is common, for example, for foster children to be part of complex sibling groups in their birth and foster families. It is also common for foster children to have complex relationships with extended birth and foster families. These relationships and the benefits and difficulties they may represent will feature strongly in the way in which social work with parents evolves. Looking at how contact arrangements emerge it is clear how much the sibling and extended family contexts can be making a difference not only to the child but also to the parent. In addition, the networks of professional agencies around the child, the placement and the birth family will also have an impact on how well family relationships operate and placements work out.

Not only within the Looked After Children review process, but at other times too, there needs to be an ecological approach. The role and attitude of the teacher, the school nurse, the doctor, the therapist, the police officer can all be having an impact on how clearly the child is seen to be part of the foster family and the birth family.

Managing permanence with parents in mind

Through the parents' and social workers' accounts of all aspects of their different and linked experiences, it was clear that the longer-term nature of children's foster placements, the majority of which were 'permanent' with no plan to return home, created particular challenges and uncertainties about the parents' identity and role as parents and the work that social workers should undertake with them.

If the aim as set out in legislation and guidance is for parents to maintain some role in their children's lives as they move though childhood and adolescence, the challenge for parents is to keep the children present and up-to-date in their own minds, while also keeping themselves as parents present and up-to-date in the minds of their children. To achieve this, parents need social workers to be both empathic and active communicators about and between the children and the parents. This means that parents need to be kept present and up-to-date in the minds of the social workers too. Shared awareness of the parents' difficulties in the past is important, but so also is awareness of the way in which children and parents may have changed over time and of the parents' current capacity to play a parenting role, even if this is only by showing their interest and concern for their children.

For case responsible social workers, the goal is, effectively, to maintain the status quo, i.e. the stability and well-being of the child in the planned permanent placement. This is not the more usual social work role as active intervener, bringing about change and then moving on. Although there is advocacy to do and arrangements to be made, about school or contact, much of the social work role falls back on more traditional practice, i.e. relationship-based work with children and families. However, although the relationship with the child and the foster carer may seem clearly aimed at making and sustaining a successful placement, work with the parents can be less clear in achieving this primary goal. On the other hand, for most fostered children, resolving their feelings about the birth family is an absolute necessity in order to thrive in placement. To the extent that parents themselves can contribute to this process, the social worker's goals for the child can be best achieved by facilitating this contribution from parents.

But there are gaps and misunderstandings in this longer-term relationship between parents and social workers. As this research suggests, most social workers recognise that the loss of children to foster care is a traumatic experience for parents. Social workers understand specifically how difficult court and contact experiences can be for parents. But, with some notable exceptions, parents do not feel understood by social workers, who are described as representing the 'authorities', being too distant, too young, too educated or as talking from a text book.

On the other hand, social workers often assume that for most parents the dominant feeling is anger, and that angry parents would not want contact from social workers. Yet for almost all parents, the emotional picture is more complex. Parents who have angry feelings about some aspects of the past are often predominantly sad and appreciate the progress children have made in foster care. They commonly accept some responsibility for the risk and harm to their children at the time they came into care, even if they feel that children might have returned to them at a later date. And even the most stuck and angry parents will become less stuck and angry if they feel that they are taken into account by social workers, provided with information and their role and identity – and feelings – are recognised. Achieving a satisfactory role for the parent does not mean increasing contact with the child or changing the balance between birth families and foster families in the child's life. But it does require the social worker to be actively engaged with the parents – and this demanding child-focussed/parent-focussed work will also require supportive, reflective supervision.

Work with the child in long-term placements planned for permanence needs to be very subtle in managing these relationships and in particular the child's need to maintain a sense of their birth family identity while gaining significantly from the life experiences – and also identity – that they may find in the foster family. It seems likely that the comfort that parents take from the maintenance of a positive idea of their role as a parent is echoed by the same need in their sons and daughters. We should not be surprised that foster children who are well-settled in their foster families continue to value the idea that they remain their parents' children and that their parents are committed to them – even if they are in mutually loving and committed relationships with foster carers and other foster family members and would not wish to return to the birth family home. This is part of the child's birth family identity that exists independent of the quality of the relationship.

It is this need in parents and children to retain certain ideas about themselves as members of a family that creates some real dilemmas for working with parents and children in foster care. How in particular do we give a message of 'permanence' to the child that feels helpful in terms of offering a sense of security in the foster placement, but does not feel unhelpful in signalling some kind of ending or marginalising of the identity and relationship with the birth family? Similarly, communicating with parents about a permanence plan can raise new concerns and anxieties about their role and identity that need to be managed.

Finally

When a child is separated from their birth family and grows up in a foster family, emotions run high and the relationships between all parties, but especially those between parents and social workers, will be complex and challenging. Perhaps one of the most important messages to come from this research is that parents vary considerably in their ability to manage their feelings, identity and situation and to contribute to the stability and welfare of their children. Parents will also in many cases change over time in many aspects of their lives, with some continuing to struggle with drugs, mental health problems, and periods of imprisonment, while others move on significantly, meet a stable partner and develop settled households, often with further children who they parent successfully. These differences are then linked to their varying ability to sustain what is a most difficult task, retaining some role as a parent when their child is being brought up by foster carers, with the last word often going to the social worker.

In developing a model of good practice, social workers need to understand and support parents well, in order to protect the long-term placement but also in order to maximise the positive contribution that parents can make to the welfare of their children through to adulthood. This requires organisations to provide social workers with the skills, the resources, the supervision and the time to build constructive relationships with parents.

References

Alpert, L.T. (2005) 'Research review: Parents' services experience – a missing element in research on foster care outcomes.' *Child and Family Social Work 10*, 361–366.

Aronson, E. (1969) 'The theory of cognitive dissonance: A current perspective.' In L. Berkowitz (ed.) *Advances in Experimental Social Psychology.* New York: Academic Press.

Beek, M. and Schofield, G. (2004a) *Providing a Secure Base in Foster Care.* London: BAAF.

Beek, M. and Schofield, G. (2004b) 'Promoting Security and Managing Risk: Contact in Long-term Foster Care.' In E. Neil and D. Howe (eds) *Contact in Adoption and Permanent Foster Care: Research, Theory and Practice.* London: BAAF, pp.124–143.

Biehal, N., Ellison, S., Baker, C. and Sinclair, I. (2010) *Belonging and Permanence: Outcomes in Long-Term Foster Care and Adoption.* London: BAAF.

Breakwell, G. (1986) *Coping with Threatened Identities.* London: Methuen.

Cleaver, H. (2000) *Fostering Family Contact: A Study of Children, Parents and Foster Carers.* London: The Stationery Office.

Crocker, J. and Quinn, D.M. (2004) 'Psychological Consequences of Devalued Identities.' In M.B. Brewer and M. Hewstone (eds) *Self and Social Identity.* Oxford: Blackwell.

Department for Children, Schools and Families (2010) *The Children Act 1989 Guidance and Regulations, Vol.2: Care Planning, Placement and Case Review.* Nottingham: DCSF.

Department for Education and Skills (2003) *Every Child Matters.* London: The Stationery Office.

Department for Education and Skills (2007) *Care Matters: Time for Change.* London: Stationery Office.

Department of Heath (1999) *Looked After Children Statistics.* London: Stationery Office.

Doka, K.J. (ed.) (1989) *Disenfranchised Grief: Recognising Hidden Sorrow.* Lexington, MA: Lexington Books.

Fahlberg, V. (2001) *A Child's Journey Through Placement.* London: BAAF.

Farmer, E., Moyers, S. and Lipscombe, J. (2004) *Fostering Adolescents.* London: Jessica Kingsley Publishers.

Festinger, L. (1957) *A Theory of Cognitive Dissonance.* Evanston, IL: Row Peterson.

Haight, W., Black, J., Mangelsdorf, S., Giorgio, G., Tata, L., Schoppe, S. and Szewczyk, M. (2002) 'Making visits better: The perspectives of parents, foster parents, and child welfare workers.' *Child Welfare 81*, 173–202.

Höjer, I. (2007) *Föräldrars röster – hur är det att ha sina barn placerade i fosterhem?* (Voices of parents whose children are placed in foster care) Stockholm: Stiftelsen Allmänna Barnhuset.

Höjer, I. (2009) 'Birth parents' perception of sharing the care of their child with foster parents.' *Vulnerable Children and Youth Studies 2*, 161–168.

Hollis, M. and Howe, D. (1987) 'Moral risks in social work.' *Journal of Applied Philosophy 4*, 123–133.

Kapp, S.A. and Propp, J. (2002) 'Client satisfaction methods: input from parents with children in foster care.' *Child and Adolescent Social Work Journal 19*, 227–245.

Kapp, S.A. and Vela, R.H. (2004) 'The unheard client: assessing the satisfaction of parents of children in foster care.' *Child and Family Social Work 9*, 197–206.

Kielty, S. (2008) 'Working hard to resist a "bad mother" label: narratives of non-resident motherhood.' *Qualitative Social Work 7*, 3, 363–379.

Kielty, S. (2009) 'Non-resident motherhood: Managing a threatened identity.' *Child and Family Social Work 13*, 32–40. First published 10 August 2007, doi: 10.1111/j.1365-2206.2007.00512.x.

Lowe, N. and Murch, M. with Borkowski, M., Weaver, A., Beckford, V. and Thomas, C. (2001) *The Plan for the Child: Adoption or Long-Term Fostering*. London: BAAF.

Macaskill, C. (2002) *Safe Contact? Children in Permanent Placement and Contact with Their Birth Relatives*. London: Russell House Publishing Ltd.

Maluccio, A.N., Fein, E. and Olmstead, K.A. (1986) *Permanency Planning for Children: Concepts and Methods*. London: Batsford.

Moldestad, B. and Skilbred, D. (2009) 'Foreldres opplevelse av et foreldreskap på avstand.' (Parenting while apart. Parents' views.) *Fontene Forskning 2*, 42–52.

Neil, E. (2007) 'Coming to terms with the loss of a child: The feelings of birth parents and grandparents about adoption and post-adoption contact.' *Adoption Quarterly 10*, 1, 1–23.

Neil, E. and Howe, D. (2004) *Contact in Adoption and Permanent Placement: Research, Theory and Practice*. London: BAAF.

Reder, P., Duncan, S. and Gray, M. (1993) *Beyond Blame, Child Abuse Tragedies Revisited*. London: Routledge.

Ribbens McCarthy, J., Edwards, R. and Gillies, V. (2000) *Making Families: Moral Tales of Parenting and Step-Parenting*. Durham: Sociology Press.

Robinson, E. (2002) 'Post-adoption grief counselling.' *Adoption and Fostering 26*, 2, 57–63.

Rowe, J., Hundleby, M. and Garnett, L. (1989) *Child Care Now: A Survey of Placement Patterns*. London: BAAF.

Schofield, G. (2000) 'Parental responsibility and parenting: the needs of accommodated children in long-term foster care.' *Child and Family Law Quarterly 12*, 4, 345–362.

Schofield, G. (2009) 'Permanence in Foster Care.' In G. Schofield and J. Simmonds (eds) *The Child Placement Handbook: Research, Policy and Practice*. London: BAAF, pp.139–158.

Schofield, G. and Beek, M. (2006) *Attachment Handbook for Foster Care and Adoption*. London: BAAF.

Schofield, G. and Beek, M. (2009) 'Growing up in foster care: providing a secure base through adolescence.' *Child and Family Social Work 14*, 3, 255–266.

Schofield, G., Beek, M., Sargent, K. and Thoburn, J. (2000) *Growing up in Foster Care*. London: BAAF.

Schofield, G., Moldestad, B., Hojer, I, Ward, E., Skilbred, D., Young, J. and Havik, T. (2010) 'Managing loss and a threatened identity: experiences of parents of children growing up in foster care and implications for social work practice.' *British Journal of Social Work*. doi: 10.1093/bjsw/bcq073.

Schofield, G. and Stevenson, O. (2009) 'Contact and Relationships Between Fostered Children and their Birth Families.' In G. Schofield and J. Simmonds (eds) *The Child Placement Handbook: Research, Policy and Practice.* London: BAAF, pp.178–202.

Schofield, G., Ward, E., Beek, M. and Sellick, C. (in preparation) *Care Planning for Permanence in Foster Care: Final Report to the Nuffield Foundation.* Norwich: University of East Anglia.

Schofield, G. and Ward, E. with Warman, A., Simmonds, J. and Butler, J. (2008) *Permanence in Foster Care – A Study of Care Planning in England and Wales.* London: BAAF.

Selwyn, J., Sturgess, W., Quinton, D. and Baxter, C. (2006) *Cost and Outcomes of Non-Infant Adoptions.* London: BAAF.

Sinclair, I. (2005) *Fostering Now: Messages from Research.* London: Jessica Kingsley Publishers.

Sinclair, I., Baker, C., Lee, J. and Gibbs, I. (2007) *The Pursuit of Permanence: A Study of the English Care System.* London: Jessica Kingsley Publishers.

Sinclair, I., Baker, C. and Wilson, K. (2005) *Foster Children: Where They Go and How They Get On.* London: Jessica Kingsley Publishers.

Skilbred, D. and Moldestad, B. (2010) 'Utfordringer i Samarbeid Mellom Foreldre Til Barn i Fosterhjem Og Saksbehandlere i Barneverntjenesten.' (Co-operation issues between child welfare and parents of children in foster care.) *Tidsskriftet Norges Barnevern 87*, 1, 33–45.

Stein, M. and Munro, E. (eds) (2008) *Young People's Transitions from Care to Adulthood: International Research and Practice.* London, Jessica Kingsley Publishers.

Thoburn, J. (1991) 'Survey Findings and Conclusions' In J. Fratter, J. Rowe, D. Sapsford and J. Thoburn (eds) *Permanent Family Placement: A Decade of Experience.* London: BAAF.

Thoburn, J. (1996) 'Psychological Parenting and Child Placement: "But we want to have our cake and eat it".' In D. Howe (ed.) *Attachment and Loss in Child and Family Social Work.* Aldershot: Avebury.

Thoburn, J., Murdoch, A. and O'Brien, A. (1986) *Permanence in Child Care.* Basil Blackwell: Oxford.

Thoburn, J., Norford, E. and Rashid, S. (2000) *Permanent Family Placement for Children of Minority Ethnic Origin.* London: Jessica Kingsley Publishers.

Thorpe, R. (1980) 'The Experiences of Parents and Children Living Apart.' In J.P. Triseliotis (ed.) *New Developments in Foster Care and Adoption.* London: Routledge.

Index